DECOLONIZING BODIES

DECOLONIZING BODIES

Stories of Embodied Resistance, Healing, and Liberation

Edited by
Carolyn Ureña
Saiba Varma

BLOOMSBURY ACADEMIC
LONDON • NEW YORK • OXFORD • NEW DELHI • SYDNEY

BLOOMSBURY ACADEMIC
Bloomsbury Publishing Plc
50 Bedford Square, London, WC1B 3DP, UK
1385 Broadway, New York, NY 10018, USA
29 Earlsfort Terrace, Dublin 2, Ireland

BLOOMSBURY, BLOOMSBURY ACADEMIC and the Diana logo are
trademarks of Bloomsbury Publishing Plc

First published in Great Britain 2024

Cover design by Adriana Brioso
Cover image: Arthur Bowen Davies, Dances, 1914 or 1915, oil on canvas. Gift of
Ralph Harman Booth, 27.158. (© Detroit Institute of Arts/Bridgeman Images)

A catalogue record for this book is available from the British Library.

Library of Congress Cataloging-in-Publication Data
Names: Ureña, Carolyn, editor. | Varma, Saiba, 1983- editor.
Title: Decolonizing bodies : stories of embodied resistance, healing and
liberation / edited by Carolyn Ureña, Saiba Varma.
Description: London ; New York : Bloomsbury Academic, 2024. |
Includes bibliographical references.
Identifiers: LCCN 2024026734 (print) | LCCN 2024026735 (ebook) |
ISBN 9781350374881 (hardback) | ISBN 9781350374874 (paperback) |
ISBN 9781350374898 (epub) | ISBN 9781350374904 (ebook)
Subjects: LCSH: Human body–Social aspects. | Capitalism–Social aspects. | Decolonization.
Classification: LCC HM636 .D39 2024 (print) | LCC HM636 (ebook) |
DDC 325/.3–dc23/eng/20240928
LC record available at https://lccn.loc.gov/2024026734
LC ebook record available at https://lccn.loc.gov/2024026735

ISBN: HB: 978-1-3503-7488-1
         PB: 978-1-3503-7487-4
         ePDF: 978-1-3503-7490-4
         eBook: 978-1-3503-7489-8

Typeset by Integra Software Services Pvt. Ltd.
Printed and bound in Great Britain

To find out more about our authors and books visit www.bloomsbury.com
and sign up for our newsletters.

*This book is an offering to the colonized and formerly colonized people of the world,
may we remember all the ways life flourishes*

CONTENTS

Chapter 6

Part III
SOVEREIGNTIES, AUTONOMIES, LIBERATION

Chapter 7

Chapter 8

Chapter 9

FIGURES

ACKNOWLEDGMENTS

This book is a product of years of shared thinking and labor—all of which began with a Zoom conversation between two strangers.

Carolyn thanks Saiba for being such a steadfast partner in challenging the norms of haste and productivity that permeate academic writing, instead embracing what has become a shared practice of calm commitment throughout our work together. This project has been a wonderful continuation of both my academic research interests as well as my administrative role at a research university, and I am grateful to Dr. Janet Tighe, my predecessor as Director of Academic Advising in the College of Arts and Sciences at UPenn, for creating time and space for the pursuit of academic projects. Thank you to my husband, Stan, our son, Rafael, my mother, Matilde, and my brother, Richard, for their love and support, and for always keeping me grounded in the present. To Dr. Nelson Maldonado-Torres, thank you for teaching me how to imagine the decolonial, with you and with Fanon. And to my colleagues, students, and friends: thank you for joining me in the pursuit and celebration of joy and ease.

Saiba thanks Carolyn for being the most incredible collaborator—patient, trusting, and insightful at every step. Thank you for going (and staying) on this journey with me and for teaching me how to protect creativity and joy in our academic work. Thanks also to Mama, Meher, Aftab, my friends, interlocutors in Kashmir from whom I continue to learn about lived decolonial practices, and my students at UCSD who continually remind me of how meaningful decolonial scholarship is in their everyday lives.

We both want to thank our contributors—Isabelle, Alexia, Mardiya, Kristine, Inshah, Poh, Xiaolu, Mika, Sanna, Andrea, Erika, and Jorge—for so generously sharing pieces of their life, work, and art with us. They embodied the spirit of co-learning and inter-being that they document. We thank them for their contributions and commitments to feminist decolonial praxis, and for inspiring many of the insights of this book about the centrality of bodies and lived experience in understanding coloniality and its undoings.

We also want to thank two anonymous reviewers at Bloomsbury who offered invaluable feedback to the proposal and first draft of the manuscript. Our editor at Bloomsbury, Olivia Dellow, has been an enthusiastic supporter and patient as we navigated multiple obstacles. We also thank Pritha Suriyamoorthy and the editorial team for all their hard work in readying the manuscript for publication.

Finally, the indefatigable and talented Bhasha Chakrabarti inspired us. Her work on feminist friendship and laboring bodies brought this volume's themes to life. We thank her for allowing her work to enrich these pages.

INTRODUCTION

Carolyn Ureña and Saiba Varma

We began imagining the project that would become *Decolonizing Bodies* in the fall of 2020. It is difficult to characterize this time, as globally, we have yet to truly process the experiences and traumas of the Covid-19 pandemic. The summer of 2020 saw massive protests against racial injustice, the swell of Covid-19, and most universities globally operating remotely. As we experienced the fear and uncertainty around the spread of the novel coronavirus, which itself brought to light the extreme injustices already built into global health and economic systems, we also found ourselves deeply committed to this project at a pace that was, and is, sustainable for us. This work recognizes and witnesses the harms done to and inscribed in bodies by colonialism and coloniality, while also offering stories of healing, resistance, and liberation for ourselves, our contributors, and our readers.

Over the past three years, we met regularly over video conference, writing in shared digital documents that live in the cloud. Our project evolved as priorities shifted in our own lives as well as those of our collaborators. Several decided to leave this project because of healthcare, caregiving, and other needs. The anxieties we intuited over email communications reminded us how difficult it is for academics to bring their full selves to any project. Rather than try to "push through" these difficulties, a mode of capitalistic knowledge production that we are writing against, we honored their and our own multiple responsibilities and commitments—from childcare and health concerns, to financial, environmental, political, and temporal constraints, to relationship commitments at "home"—that we carry with us as scholars (Günel, Varma, and Watanabe 2020). Honoring those bumps and fissures became important to us, as the emotional heart of this project continues to be decolonizing academic knowledge.

Just as the pandemic shed a harsh, bright light on the inequities and injustices in our world that demand our collective attention, it also illuminated the physical, affective, and psychological demands that burden so many of us. In the wake of lockdowns and quarantines, we could rethink what is essential and necessary and forcefully say "no" to practices harmful to our own well-being. In this spirit, we hope that the openness with which we have approached this project will shine through as you approach the collection. Internally, between ourselves, we checked in periodically about what this project meant to us and whether it continued to pull our interest. At times, as we confronted challenges in our own lives, we paused our work. At other times, we see-sawed responsibilities back and forth as one or the other was overwhelmed. We negotiated our time and capacity by communicating openly with each other, and in the process, a central refrain emerged: *we do this work because we want to*. *Decolonizing Bodies* is a pleasure project for us, and we insistently maintained that sense of joy in our collaboration. Throughout the process of writing, we remained compelled to bring this work to life because the question of decolonizing bodies remained—and still remains—important to us, both personally and intellectually. Our collection is a small contribution to an ongoing conversation about what it means to witness and acknowledge the way bodies tell stories—to ourselves and to others—the way our world attempts to limit what is possible, and how decolonial embodiments and embodied knowledge can show us many new and promising paths forward (Please see also Walsh 2023).

In our process as well as in the volume, we hope to provide a model for what engaged and accessible scholarship can look like. The pieces in this collection are written in a range of voices—some are more traditionally academic, others are memoirs or personal essays, while still others are mixed-genre. This unapologetic boundary jumping is intended to open up questions about the legacy of colonialism in academia and the world, including how we write, and for whom. In so doing, we are mindful of Cusicanqui's critique of how struggles and discourses of decolonization have been appropriated by scholars located in the global North, isolating "academic treatises from any obligation to or dialogue with insurgent social forces" (2012: 98). These "myriad" offerings are intended to suit the needs and appetites of differently positioned readers (Mani 2023). Whether you, as a reader, experience moments of recognition or disorientation,[1] we hope you will feel called into the conversation and make your own contributions to what decolonizing bodies may mean for you. For us, the multiplicity of offerings that comprise *Decolonizing Bodies* are more than aesthetic choices; they are also necessary political interventions that decenter the written word as the authoritative enactment of voice.

Decolonizing Bodies shows how Black, Indigenous, racialized, colonized, disabled, mad, and queer people survive multiple systems of oppression, actively resist colonial presents, and build spaces of liberation, autonomy, and sovereignty through bodily practices. Following Cusicanqui, our collection affirms that "there can be no discourse of decolonization, no theory of decolonization, without a decolonizing practice" (2012: 100). Specifically, our contributors offer novel theorizations of how interlocking systems of racial capitalism, colonialism, and heteropatriarchal violence erode the bodily schema and experiences of racialized and colonized populations globally, while being equally attentive to how racialized

---

1. We note that *dis*-orientation, following the feminist philosopher Sara Ahmed (2006), can be a generative experience to think with and think from.

and colonized people live and confront these displacements and disintegrations. In our analysis, racism and colonialism are alive in people's skins. They sediment as bodily and habitual practices, which are active, ongoing, made, and remade. Bodies, we argue, powerfully register the impacts of colonial and racialized violence, but through practices of embodiment, they also digest, expel, and transform them.

A Word about Decoloniality

In contrast to postcolonial theory, which began as a response to the end of British colonialism and is in genealogical succession to both post-structuralism and postmodernism, "decolonial thinking and doing emerged and unfolded, from the sixteenth century on, as responses to the oppressive and imperial bent of modern European ideals projected to and enacted in, the non-European world" (Mignolo 2011: 3). This longer view of history widens our scope of inquiry and encourages returning to embodied narratives and experiences that have been rendered suspect by Eurocentrism and post-structuralism alike. Mignolo's challenge, then, is to "think decolonially" by confronting "all of Western civilization, which includes liberal capitalism and Marxism," specifically "from the perspective of the colonies and ex-colonies rather than from the perspective internal to Western civilization itself" (Mignolo 2011: xviii). In this way, coloniality can be understood as co-constitutive of modernity and witnessed as ongoing oppression and alienation inflicted upon those exploited in the name of modernity, even into the present postcolonial era.

"Decolonizing bodies" as a frame attends to ongoing decolonization processes in politics, education, and our everyday lives that occur at the level of the body. It highlights how nonnormative and distinct bodies contribute new knowledge and practices that remake the world. Our efforts are very much in conversation with Walsh's efforts to "crack coloniality," to reveal, as she puts it, "fissures in this totalizing system or matrix of power, and to widen further the fissures that already exist in coloniality's supposedly impenetrable wall." As she notes, these fissures are often available to us at the level of "situated and embodied questions" (Walsh 2023: 7). We hope that you will join us in celebrating all bodies and the knowledge they produce.

Bodies That Speak: Revisiting Embodiment

Embodiment describes the experience of having, being, and thinking in a body. Questions of embodiment are central to many fields—feminist, gender and sexuality studies, critical race and ethnic studies, disability studies, medical anthropology, art history, philosophy, and feminist science and technology studies, among others. This work has challenged hegemonic Euro-American notions of a split between body and mind and of the individual body as a separate, bounded, and sovereign entity. In imagining "decolonizing bodies," our initial goal was to intervene in studies of embodiment in the humanities and social sciences by foregrounding decolonial thought. We were inspired by Ureña's prior writing on decolonial embodiment, particularly her interest in decolonial healing, which emphasizes "the necessarily *ongoing* practice of healing, a process which need not even be realized in order to remain a worthwhile venture" (2019: 1644).

This perspective on healing has a troubled, if not incompatible, relationship with Western medicine (biomedicine), which not only promotes a curative model but has historically understood and treated the mind and body as separate entities. As described by Ryle (1949: 11–12), biomedicine imagines that "a person ... lives through two collateral histories, one comprising of what happens in and to the body, the other consisting of what happens in and to the mind." Biomedicine, like our contemporary medical industrial complex, views human beings through materialist and reductionist frameworks, as biological organisms that can be understood by examining their constituent parts. In this worldview, disease is seen as a deviation from biological norms, whereas health is defined as an absence of disease. This definition contravenes most of the world's healing systems (Mehta 2011).

By attending to the historical and ongoing entanglements between colonial violence and biomedicine and how they impact the bodies of colonized and racialized people, this volume offers a potent critique of medical knowledge and mind-body dualism. Beyond more obvious histories of scientific racism and eugenics, medical knowledge continues to marginalize or exclude of knowledges and cultures deemed primitive or nonrational. There is a long and well-documented history of how biomedicine has historically and continually neglected nonnormative, disabled, gendered, colonized, and racialized bodies. From the unequal distribution of palliative care in the global South, to the persistence of medical racism and ableism in the global North, Black, brown, and "Other" bodies have, through their encounters with biomedical systems, been systematically dis-embodied and told that their bodily experiences don't matter, that they don't know what they are feeling, or that they do not know how to communicate their pain in appropriate, quantifiable terms.[2] In psychiatry,

---

2. In his essay, "The 'North African Syndrome,'" Frantz Fanon argued that biomedicine, particularly when intertwined with colonialism, renders colonized patients and their bodies illegible. From the perspective of medical providers, the North African body arrives "enveloped in vagueness," Fanon writes, not due to a "lack of comprehension" on the part of doctors, but because of a profound ontological gap between the physician and patient. Because of the histories of colonization and mistrust that shape the clinical encounter, patients are unable to be understood on their own terms. The patient does not feel at home in the clinic, it is not a space that belongs to them. Rather, the clinic is an extension of the colonial apparatus. These conditions produce a recalcitrant, vague, or, in many cases, silent patient. As Fanon writes, it is only by accounting for the close connections between biomedicine, colonialism, and history that we have any hope of penetrating the patient's silence. Fanon, *Toward the African Revolution*, 7.

patients in the majority world who express psychological distress in and through physiological symptoms—that is, who do not conform to "mind-body" dualism—are often labeled with their own psychiatric disorder, somatization, which serves to further pathologize their lived experiences.

We are encouraged by some signs from medicine, public health, and related fields that things are slowly changing. Indeed, interest in investigating the links between biological processes and "social determinants of health" is at an all-time high. This work has made space for new understandings of embodiment that derive from outside the ivory towers of the medical-industrial complex. For example, the rise of functional and integrative medicine, as well as the popularity of non-biomedical therapeutics in the global North, seeks to incorporate etiological factors such as diet, nutrition, lifestyle, relationships, and environmental exposure into treatment protocols. Similarly, trauma-informed psychiatry and psychology are integrating somatic techniques such as meditation and mindfulness with trauma therapy (Van der Kolk 1994; Rothschild 2000). These practices can help those who have experienced trauma and harm reclaim their bodies.[3] This work shows how embodiment, as a framework and a set of practices, can speak back to hegemonic epistemologies of the body that prioritize physiological etiologies of disease, assume and produce normativity and standardization, and value some bodies over others.

Our work builds on this burgeoning movement within medicine while also offering something beyond it. First, most of our contributors write from their own lived experiences—as Indigenous, colonized, queer, mad, sick, or disabled people—who are responding to the toxic remains of racial capitalism and colonialism in their own bodies and reclaiming their excluded subjectivities and voices. Second, and relatedly, they reveal how the embodied effects of colonial violence exist beyond their physiological, biological, or genetic expressions (i.e., the "biology of trauma"). Our volume goes beyond the traditional markers of pathology to effectively explore traumas and wounds occasioned by lived experiences of coloniality. Third, our work foregrounds the political potential of the body and of embodied practices to remake selves, relations, and communities in the midst or aftermath of devastating violence.

The bodies of Black, Indigenous, colonized, disabled, gendered, and racialized people reveal hidden histories of colonialism and alert us to how colonial processes have disrupted, interrupted, or transformed modes of embodiment. What languages of distress or vernacular theories of power might emerge from these bodily histories? As Rupa Marya and Raj Patel put it, "colonialism isn't simply the physical occupation of land. It is a process, an operation of power in which one cosmology is extinguished and replaced with another. In that replacement, one set of interpretations about humans' place in the universe is supplanted. Patterns of identity, language, culture, work, relationship, territory, time, community and care

---

3. This work also shows that disembodiment can be a survival mechanism when we have experienced physical trauma or harm.

are transformed" (Marya and Patel 2021: 14). By centering the ongoing impacts of colonial violence on the body and the efforts of colonized and racialized communities to grapple with these histories through decolonial praxes, this collection heralds a major shift in embodiment studies, which generally takes the white, cis-male, able-bodied person as its unmarked subject.

As the British-Palestinian writer Isabella Hammad describes, in colonial histories, "so much that happens is not recorded–not caught on paper or photographed, or else the traces are not considered worthy of saving or are destroyed or skewed" (Hammad 2023). *Decolonizing Bodies* is an effort to redefine and salvage those traces, and where they do not exist, to meditate on their absences and silences. In this volume, readers will bear witness to the "enormous wound" (Fanon 1964: 48) of coloniality expressed through a range of disordered bodily experiences and expressions, including shock, fear, anxiety, and "burnout." While these experiences have a physiological component, they are not circumscribed by it. Bodily wounds are eloquent, calling out for acknowledgment, recognition, or understanding (Whitehead 1999). The relational forms of embodiment highlighted both reflect histories of collective struggle and illuminate those histories in a new way.

Our book also honors histories and philosophies of embodiment that exist outside Euro-American genealogies. Within academia, the "discovery" of embodiment theory is often credited to the twentieth-century French phenomenologist Maurice Merleau-Ponty. Nêhiyaw and Saulteaux scholar Margaret Kovach, however, notes how Western phenomenology has historically not attended to political and colonial dimensions of experience (2009: 39) or to "holistic epistemologies that emphasize self-knowledge" (2009: 111). By contrast, Sufi, Tantric, Buddhist, and other Indigenous epistemologies have long emphasized the body as a site of awareness and knowledge. These knowledges do not conceptualize the individual as a bounded, discrete entity. Instead, concepts such as interdependence foreground the multiple and myriad relationalities at the heart of embodiment (Mani 2023). In the poetic words of the physician and Zen priest Jan Chozen Bays (2015), embodiment is "interpenetration of what I call me and what I call paper just now as I read,/ interpenetration of what I call me and what I call carpet felt, walls seen, air breathed, trees outside, continuously creating each other, mutual verification, no/ distance at all … /"

Echoing these profound insights, our contributors meditate on embodiment in relation to spirits, ancestors, plants, kin, and comrades, to show how our being is always already enmeshed in and affected by other, as well as with the nonhuman world. To borrow from another Zen Buddhist teacher, Thich Nhat Hanh, we "*inter-are*." These epistemologies also make space for the sacredness and integrity of all life forms. As filmmaker and postcolonial theorist Lata Mani describes, Indigenous and non-Western philosophies invite "intimacy with all that exists," aligning us with "the nature of creation as a nonhierarchical interdependence, egalitarian polyexistence" (2023: 33). This approach can also highlight how struggles for liberation are not abstract, disembodied political endeavors, but are waged—as the works of many of our contributors show—on psychic, bodily, existential, phenomenological, and cosmological registers—all at once.

Collectively, *Decolonizing Bodies* moves us away from accounts of individual, bounded, able-bodied, normal, sovereign subjects toward viewing bodies as porous, relational, and instrumental in collective struggle, including in the ongoing work of decolonization. As Ureña puts it, "Embodiment [is] an essential source of knowledge for those in need of a guiding light in a world stricken by violence and alienation" (2019: 1641). Bodies have communicative capacities that exceed language (see Derges 2009). This is shown in Mika Lior's essay about *samba de roda*, a ritualized dance performed by Caboclos, practitioners of Candomblé, a syncretic African Diasporic religion established by enslaved and free Afro-descendent actors brought to Brazil through the transatlantic slave trade. Embodiment has worldmaking possibilities.

Fanon and "Nonbeing"

One of our intellectual ancestors in understanding the impacts of colonialism on racialized and colonized bodies is the revolutionary Black Martinican clinician and philosopher Frantz Fanon, who served as a psychiatrist for the French colonial state in Algeria. As a psychiatrist, the inadequate care, harms, and negligence woven into Fanon's practice due to being enmeshed in a colonial system, transformed him. As a physician working for the French colonial administration, his own body operated as an extension of the colonial state ("in the colonies, the doctor is an integral part of colonization, of domination, of exploitation," he writes (1964: 134)).

In his later writings, Fanon revealed the limits of biomedical psychiatry to heal the "enormous wound" (1964: 48) of colonial oppression. One example of this "enormous wound" is conveyed through the idea of ontological "nonbeing." In *Black Skin, White Masks*, Fanon describes how the white gaze "fixes" Black bodies, leaving them without the possibility of attaining full personhood or bodily experience, since they are always already reduced to being a distorted reflection/ Other. In tracing the lived experiences of racialization and colonization, following Fanon, we prioritize racialized embodiments—the lived experiences of those designated as "nonbeings." Our collection shows how racialized and colonized subjects continue to experience and be seen as "nonbeing(s)" through existing social institutions and dominant historical frameworks which fail to adequately discern, diagnose, or recognize the ongoing effects of colonialism.

Readers will experience the effects of "nonbeing" in a number of different settings—in the archive of the Library of Congress, where Isabelle Higgins' search for the bodies of Black children from the 1860s to the 1920s leads to the discovery of an absence, reminding her of her own difficulties of being a fully bodied researcher, to the calls for disappearance that queer Muslim online creators experience in both online and offline worlds that Mardiya Siba Yahaya documents, to the everyday, gendered disruptions to movement and subjectivity experienced by generations of Kashmiri Muslim women, as chronicled by Inshah Malik. "Nonbeing" as an analytic and phenomenological process attends to both anti-Black and anti-Muslim racism, while being enfleshed in each specific context. The result is a new enactment of embodiment studies that does not take the body's ontology, material presence, or knowability for granted.

Beyond "Damage-Centered" Research

Colonial regimes of power operate through, and reinforce, linear, capitalist, and settler colonial notions of time and place, capitalistic logics of individualism, extraction, and productivity, and biomedical norms of illness, such as those which posit disability as loss or cure as restoration to a previous state of being. Both capitalist and colonial regimes of labor—in the factory or prison, to use two foundational examples—objectify and organize laboring bodies, readying them for maximal extraction of value. Within these conditions, "bodies of color continue to be necessary to the maintenance of the bio-necropolitical order and its extraction of resources and labor for symbolic and material profit" (Khanmalek and Rhodes 2020: 37; see also Vora 2015). And as many of our contributors show, colonized and racialized people internalize these systems of oppression (see Arani, this volume; Nandy 1983 [2009]).

In attending to colonial violence in our bodies, this collection is mindful not to reproduce what the Unangax̂ scholar Eve Tuck (2009) calls "damage-centered research." Decolonial scholars have moved away from thinking of colonialism as an event toward understanding it as a process—one that continues to live in bodies, relations, environments, and social life. These scholars have also highlighted resurgences, shifts, and movements of "decoloniality in/as praxis." Beyond merely responding to or documenting a colonial past, our work reimagines past, present, and future possibilities for subjects and communities engaged in the processual work of decolonizing. Attending to what bodies *do* helps make visible how the time of the decolonial is not in an abstract, subjunctive future, but is folded into the present. Bodies, we show, can remake history.

Bodies Are Portals to Healing Worlds

Decolonizing Bodies explores how people creatively remake and transform multiple forms of oppression through practices like resting, performing, studying, planting, dancing, praying, and storytelling. For us, the "here and now" of decolonizing practices is extremely important to bear witness to, in the midst of ongoing capitalist and colonial devastation. Bodies are portals to healing worlds.

The word "healing" is derived from the same root as the word "whole." Healers recognize the phenomenological and existential dimensions of suffering and understand the importance of reintegrating lifeworlds. In the words of the Guyanese-Danish new media artist Tabita Rezaire (2022: 152), "to overcome the disconnection to ourselves, to each other, to the earth, and the universe mandated by coloniality, the healing we require is not solely physical nor mental but emotional, political, historical, technological, and spiritual." This collection connects these registers of healing without drawing sharp boundaries between them, since, for all of our contributors, emotional, political, historical, and technological healing are co-imbricated. For example, in Mardiya Siba Yahaya's piece, the social media platform TikTok offers queer Muslim persons liberatory possibilities for self-expression, yet Yahaya contextualizes those within ongoing capitalist and colonial practices of invasive data collection and surveillance by big tech. Likewise, in two chapters on gardening—from two different corners of the world—engagements with the nonhuman world, and plants in particular, help colonized communities "access another dimension, a vegetal reality, where we experience the subtle layers of existence" (Rezaire 2022: 155). In urban gardens in Bogotá and Srinagar that are created and maintained through women's labor and knowledge, the ever-pushing temporality of capitalist and colonial extraction pauses. In Mattoo and Varma's photo essay, Rubia, a third-generation Kashmiri gardener confesses that she could spend "all day in the garden, if she got the chance." The garden is an escape and respite for the women who tend to it, but it is also a site of communal care.

In the pages that follow, unapologetically creative and literary lexicons respond to the subtle, invisible, indirect effects of colonialism. Bodies dance, fight, labor, laugh, tell stories, struggle, and love, expanding our collective imagination and repertoire of how lifeworlds, bodies, and collectivities engage in decolonial practices.

Structure

The collection is organized in three parts. We begin with pieces that document neglected traces of colonial and capitalist violence, particularly on the bodies of our multiply situated researchers. Next, our contributors examine relational and collective decolonial practices, showing how negotiations of bodily reclamations occur within contexts of ongoing coloniality. Finally, the pieces that close the volume explore examples of decolonial world-building through intimacy with the nonhuman world. Each section of the book begins with a visual work by the South Asian American artist Bhasha Chakrabarti. Chakrabarti's work highlights the key themes of our collection—the politics of knowledge (Kali/tongues), the relationality of bodies (Intertwining), and the critical feminist labor of sowing, mending, and healing. We invite you to rest and meditate on these works in relation to the pieces that follow them.

Part I: Decolonizing Research

The essays in Part I expose, critique, and challenge how "traditional" models of doing research, knowing, and relating to our "subjects" are mired in coloniality. In archives and during ethnographic fieldwork, colonial ways of knowing appear as binary, often gendered subject/object relationships that prioritize objectivity and rationality as the bearers of knowledge, whereas those deemed subjective or irrational are dismissed or "explained away." Colonial practices of knowledge creation also starkly separate research and activism, emotion and knowledge, resulting in depoliticized or disembodied discussions that alienate those outside academia.

The essays in Part I powerfully reorient dominant epistemologies in the social sciences away from modes of coloniality toward decolonial practices and goals. These pieces reflect upon the bidirectional, interdependent relationship between the authors and the communities with whom they engage. The authors, all of whom occupy "multiple consciousnesses" (Harrison 1991)—as racialized and/or queer community organizers and social scientists—use their multiple positionings and identities as strengths. Their inhabiting of dual, and sometimes multiple, worlds allows them to examine and demystify research by showing us experiences usually hidden from view. In so doing, they destabilize the idea that research produces knowledge about the "Other," and instead use it as a form of self-knowledge and self-transformation, albeit one that may be laced with traumatic experiences in the form of anxiety, fear, and burnout. Through haunting auto/ethnographic histories, which offer a window into their self-discovery, almost in real time, our contributors grapple with the complexity of how they are impacted by their daily work, whether community organizing or archival research. By making themselves the objects of research, they shed light on the way coloniality resides even in the privileged bodies of researchers. In each of these essays, personal, intellectual, and political stakes become clear, as each "knower" is transformed by their work.

What emerges from these accounts is how the everyday violences of research are embodied, gendered, and invisibilized to enable research itself. These pieces offer us deeply felt and carefully theorized accounts of the ableist assumptions undergirding productivity in academia, the mental health impacts of doing research and writing work, and the way extra demands of undoing historical wrongs fall on the bodies of queer people and people of color. They powerfully shed light on the ways decolonial research must theorize the interconnections between intimate, personal, political, and material concerns. We hope these examples motivate other practitioners to reevaluate the prescribed and sanctioned ways of being during and beyond the research encounter and to expand the frame of what counts *as* research or knowledge. In each case, these writers demonstrate care for their work, which is simultaneously an act of repair and caregiving—to themselves and to communities intimate and ancestral. What comes to light is the need for researchers engaged in decolonial projects to care for themselves, in order to engage ethically and effectively in their commitments.

In "Complex Connections: Coloniality, Embodiment, and Children of Colour in the Archives," Isabelle Higgins recounts a recent research fellowship experience at the Library of Congress, where she spent six months searching for images of children of color created and produced for late nineteenth-century white audiences. Drawing on her own embodied experiences of pain, haunting, and trauma as well as decolonial theory, she asks what role her experiences as a self-described "mixed-race white British and Afro-Caribbean" who is white-passing played in disrupting or reproducing the colonial matrix of power.

Alexia Arani's "Burnout: A Queer Femme of Color Auto-Ethnography" likewise engages in a narrative of deep self-reflection, drawing our attention to the very real costs, both physical and psychological, of engaging in activist work as a researcher. In this beautifully rendered auto-theoretical and auto-ethnographic portrait of burnout, Arani shares fieldnotes from their dissertation work which reveal the real and often unacknowledged challenges and costs of maintaining balance and well-being for themselves while supporting others in a community of queer and trans people of color.

Part II: Decolonizing Collectives

If Part I foregrounds the embodied experiences of researchers in their encounters with coloniality, Part II emphasizes communal practices that retell and rework the past. Historical pasts of violence, oppression, and colonialism make themselves particularly felt. Colonial pasts are not abstract, but intimately lived, known, and most importantly, *remade* through modes of storytelling. Just as the past is not merely past, so too is the colonial not easily separable from the decolonial. The reclamations of decolonial stories, histories, performances, and ways of being in this section coexist with structures of coloniality. Without reproducing neat binaries of resistance/oppression, our contributors attend to the tenuous ways that marginalized communities fashion themselves and their loved ones and find room to breathe within oppressive structures. Through Indigenous practices of intergenerational storytelling ("Decolonized Bodies of Land and Children" and "Embodying Azadi"), Muslim queer and trans practices of self-fashioning online ("Existing Beyond Time and Space: Understanding Queer Muslim Visibilities Online"), and narrative therapy ("Fragments Contain Worlds"), bodies become sites of inhabiting, in the etymological sense of *habitare*, complex histories of colonial and decolonial becoming.

History dwells in stories, where cultivated conscious and unconscious practices of liberatory self and communal knowing can be found. Each of these pieces offers us inspiring accounts of bodies and stories in motion. Storytelling as a communal practice can take many forms, such as when an individual makes their own autobiographical narrative a vehicle for inspiring political action, or when a queer or trans Muslim creator uses online mediums to re-create notions of home or belonging, and in so doing, invites a broader community to identify and empathize with experiences made familiar and recognizable across cultural differences. At other times, storytelling can be a way of retelling history to ourselves to make sense of the world around us by first making sense of our own family.

By grounding decolonial bodily praxes in scenes of intimate life, which increasingly include digital mediums, these chapters also offer compelling new theorizations of the body. Rather than singular, self-contained entities, bodies emerge as multiply constituted, in the words of Lee (this volume), not as a single entity or story, but rather "as a diverse community of different members, each with their own relationships, histories, positions, and experiences." Similarly, Mardiya Siba Yahaya chronicles the ways queer Muslim TikTok users use the medium to create and navigate multiple selves and identities—both online and offline—as they negotiate their own safety, security, and need for self-expression. Decolonial praxes are highly relational and co-constitutive, whether through Inshah Malik's account of her own subjectivity and personhood emerging in and through her relationships with her maternal elders, in Kristine Koyama's description of Sarah Winnemucca's call on her audience to feel the pain of loss experienced by members of her community, or in Xiaolu and Poh's exchanges about creativity and process which displace the hierarchy between "therapist" and "client."

In "Existing Beyond Time and Place: Understanding Queer Muslim Visibilities Online," Mardiya Siba Yahaya's search for queer Muslims leads to an exploration of the potential and limitations of the "digital body" in allowing for self-representation and communal acceptance. As Yahaya writes, the online world allows for "queer digital counterpublics … that allow queer people to craft their identities" and at the same time, these spaces are not uniformly safe or free from violence. By attending to regimes of surveillance, violence, control, and commodification of queer and trans bodies and experiences online, Yahaya shows us how queer Muslim online users across the African continent express "rage, pain, activism, and solidarity, alongside joy and satire." Users simultaneously dismantle hetero- and homo-normative ideals—for example, the assumption that it is impossible to be both queer and Muslim—through always careful and calibrated acts of creativity and agency online.

Kristine Koyama's "Decolonized Bodies of Land and Children: How Sarah Winnemucca Affected Political Action in the Nineteenth Century" draws on Indigenous critical scholarship as well as the power of storytelling to reveal how Indigenous bodies unsettle colonial violence and expand how scholars historicize Indigenous rights movements today. Specifically, their piece examines Paiute author and activist Sarah Winnemucca's 1883 autobiography *Life Among the Piutes*, a coming-of-age narrative that Koyama argues succeeds in transforming nineteenth-century readers' embodied knowledge and making them feel invested in Winnemucca's political project of restoring Indigenous land to its original inhabitants.

Inshah Malik's essay, "Embodying Azadi: Conscious and Unconscious Womanhood in Indian Occupied Kashmir," traces how three generations of women from both sides of Malik's family are living repositories of Kashmir's colonial and anti-colonial histories. She shows how storytelling, including stories of spiritual knowledge and practice drawn from Sufi traditions, operates as a crucial site of everyday, decolonial feminist praxis. Malik's essay powerfully correlates Aurora Morales's argument of women's testimonials as "histerimonias," because, as she writes, "'testimonio' comes from the custom of Roman men swearing on their testicles … and because the idea of hysteria has been used for many centuries to dismiss and silence those who are considered unreliable witnesses, especially women" (2019: 48). Malik beautifully ties her own self-fashioning as a feminist intellectual to relations with significant male and female persons in her life, demonstrating how our bodies are multitudes.

Poh Lin Lee and Xialou Wang's strikingly original and transporting piece, "Fragments Contain Worlds: Encounters between Bodies," invites readers to witness—visually and in writing—their ongoing conversations about Xialou's process-driven filmmaking and Poh's anti-oppressive narrative therapy practice. By offering us glimpses into their movingly constructed dialogue, they invite an audience to experience the multiplicity of bodies not merely as a theoretical tool, but as a practical orientation for healing. Fragments of embedded video accompany their own creative writing, and in so doing, they encourage audiences to bring an experiential spirit to the encounter, to begin to unravel the modes of colonial thinking that might be stymying our own creative processes.

Part III: Sovereignties, Autonomies, Liberation

While Part II focuses on negotiations, contestations, and reclamations, in Part III we enter places of freedom, autonomy, and liberation that are thriving in spaces of colonialism and coloniality. To paraphrase Andrea Sánchez-Castañeda, Erika Nivia, and Jorge Yopasá, these pieces attend to the presence of "seeds in cities of cement." Here, seeds and cement are not mere metaphors. In each of the pieces in Part III, multiply marginalized and colonized communities engage in grounded, bodily practices to fight material, social, and epistemic dispossession. As decolonial theorists and practitioners have long argued, autonomy is not a fixed structure or framework, but a *process*, here embodied as Indigenous dance traditions in Brazil ("Ele gosta do samba rasgado") and urban gardens in Kashmir and Colombia. While each of these practices and their participants differ in scale and degree of formal organization, they nonetheless serve as powerful examples of *territorios en resistencia* ("territories in resistance," Zibechi 2008) in their commitments to recuperating land, remaining autonomous from the state and political affiliations, affirming cultural identities, and cultivating relationships with nature.

The contributions to Part III center on non-Anglophone, Indigenous perspectives and practices regarding the interdependence and interrelation of the human and the nonhuman, thereby disrupting the often hierarchical dynamics that are themselves the result of the coloniality of knowledge. As Walter Mignolo once described, decolonial liberation is the process of creating new forms of community life. These pieces show us how decolonial liberation often spring from our intimacy with the nonhuman world. These themes are poignantly highlighted throughout this part of the collection, particularly in "A Garden of Im/Possibility," where Varma writes:

> *Remove the gardeners*
> *and what happens to the garden?*

And later,

> To care, in this way, is to decolonize:
> not to dismantle, but to create.

In exploring the relationship between human practitioners of caboclo, Lior's piece highlights the permeability of human and spirit worlds. In centering the role of urban gardens as *"aulas vivas,"* or living classrooms, the piece by Sánchez-Castañeda, Nivia, and Yopasá signals the pedagogical significance and the ability of these spaces to influence human behavior, just as they, too, are impacted by human action or inaction. Human intervention in nature promotes life in a symbiotic relationship. Even the language used by our contributors, who view their contribution as "nourish[ing] a more heterodox urban political ecology," signals how variously life sustaining a caring decolonial practice can be. These examples deepen our existing understandings of concepts such as liberation and autonomy by showing how the labor *and* bodily pleasure of women and nonbinary people are critical to the *processes* and practices of decolonization—dancing, singing, socializing, gardening, and dreaming.

Mika Lior's "'Ele gosta do samba rasgado' ('He likes a rough samba'): Ceremonial embodiments of Bahian Candomblé Caboclo" is based on extensive fieldwork in the Bahia region of Brazil, which has been formative for the development of the syncretic Afro-Brazilian religion of Candomblé, as well as the expressive genres of samba and capoeira. Lior's essay addresses ritual choreographies as relational ways of knowing, suggesting that practitioners of Candomblé embody complex histories of struggle through their ritual choreographies, while also developing new ways of understanding those histories by drawing on social, racial, and sexual marginalization as sources of ritual power and efficacy.

"A Garden in a Lake of Im/Possibility" is a beautiful visual ethnographic poem in which Saiba Varma and Sanaa Irshad Matto's text and photographs work together to offer a complex and moving account of the "centuries-old feminist praxis of gardening on Dal Lake, one of Kashmir's most historically significant, but also most ecologically fragile and vulnerable tourist attractions, located in the heart of Srinagar city." This piece serves to draw our attention to the relationships between people, plants, and rapidly changing urban environments.

"Quyca chiahac chixisqua [Sowing ourselves in the territory]: embodied experiences of Indigenous urban gardens and the coloniality of nature" is a multi-authored piece written by Andrea Sánchez-Castañeda, Erika Nivia Fuentes, and Jorge David Yopasá Cárdenas. They offer a deeply engaging view of the Muysca practice of urban gardening in Colombia, with an eye toward the gendered labor that sustains it, as well as how and why these gardens are significant spaces in which to think about decoloniality. The authors shed light on the significance of Indigenous urban gardens as sites of resistance that function as living classrooms, serving to sustain communities by providing nourishing food and supporting Indigenous language preservation. This chapter and Kristine

Koyama's earlier chapter exemplify a decolonial feminist geographical approach that foregrounds the relationship between land and embodiment, what Sofia Garagocin and Martina Angela Caretta (2019) describe as cuerpo-territorio, the inseparable ontological relationship between body and territory. This approach centers Indigenous knowledge, which in turn reminds us of the material stakes of decolonial efforts.

A Note about Us

While working in different disciplines, as co-editors of this diverse collection we connected through our shared interests in colonialism, medicine, and decolonial theory. Together, we both felt an urgent need in the social sciences and humanities to offer novel theorizations of the body from the perspective of racialized and colonized communities *and* to account for the creative work of decolonization that is ongoing. By working with and drawing from fields across disciplinary divides, we believe in the potential of those who have previously been rendered voiceless to create alternative futures.

My (Ureña's) approach to embodiment studies draws in large part from my research on the medical and political writings of Frantz Fanon. As a multilingual comparatist working at the intersection of the humanities and the medical sciences, my approach to embodiment studies is grounded in literary analysis. In my broader engagement with Fanon, I argue that reading literature with Fanon allows us to see why we need new narratives of the human, and why we need to focus our attention on the wounding legacies of slavery and colonialism. In doing so, I affirm the significance of literature to the project of promoting social justice.

As a medical and psychological anthropologist, my (Varma's) interest in decoloniality and embodiment comes from more than fifteen years of research in Kashmir, the site of a more than 450-year struggle for decolonization. While my research was initially imagined as a project on mental health—Kashmir has one of the world's highest rates of traumatic stress and PTSD—I soon came to realize that any account of mental health was incomplete without a deep reckoning with Kashmir's colonial history and present (see Varma 2020). Through grounded, ethnographic research, my work documents not only colonialism's many effects on psyches, bodies, and social landscapes, but also dwells on the embodied practices—of care, generosity, and hospitality—that people living under colonization use for their survival and thrivance.

In documenting and celebrating anti-imperial and anti-capitalist refusals in the body, our work offers ethnographic and grounded theorizing from many parts of the world. As we continue to deepen our understanding of the ongoing effects of coloniality, racism, and systems of carcerality in our own lives, we hope our collection will alert readers to the bubbling presence of creative bodily techniques, practices of resistance, and possibility all around us.

Bibliography

Ahmed, Sara. *Queer Phenomenology: Orientations, Objects, Others.* Durham and London: Duke University Press, 2006.

Bays, Jan Chozen. "Embodiment." November 17, 2015. https://tricycle.org/article/embodiment/ (accessed May 23, 2023).

Cusicanqui, Silvia Rivera. "*Ch'ixinakax utxiwa*: A Reflection on the Practices and Discourses of Decolonization." Trans. Brenda Baletti. *The South Atlantic Quarterly* 111, no. 1 (2012): 95–109.

Derges, Jane. "Eloquent Bodies: Conflict and Ritual in Northern Sri Lanka." *Anthropology and Medicine* 16, no. 1 (2009): 27–36.

Fanon, Frantz. *Toward the African Revolution: Political Essays.* New York: Grove Press, 1964.

Günel, Gökçe, Saiba Varma, and Chika Watanabe. "A Manifesto for Patchwork Ethnography." 2020. https://culanth.org/fieldsights/a-manifesto-for-patchwork-ethnography (accessed May 9, 2023).

Hammad, Isabella. "Isabella Hammad Interviewed by Feroz Rather." *Bomb* magazine. 2023. https://bombmagazine.org/articles/isabella-hammad-interviewed-2/ (accessed May 13, 2023).

Harrison, Faye V., ed. *Decolonizing Anthropology: Moving Further toward an Anthropology for Liberation.* Arlington, VA: American Anthropological Association, 1991.

Khanmalek, Tala, and Heidi Andrea Restrepo Rhodes. "A Decolonial Feminist Epistemology of the Bed: A Compendium Incomplete of Sick and Disabled Queer Brown Femme Bodies of Knowledge." *Frontiers: A Journal of Women Studies* 41, no. 1 (2020): 35–58.

Kovach, Margaret. *Indigenous Methodologies: Characteristics, Conversations, and Contexts.* Toronto: University of Toronto Press, 2009.

Mani, Lata. *Myriad Intimacies.* Durham and London: Duke University Press, 2023.

Marya, Rupa, and Raj Patel. *Inflamed: Deep Medicine and the Anatomy of Injustice.* New York: Farrar, Straus and Giroux, 2021.

Mehta, Neeta. "Mind-Body Dualism: A Critique from a Health Perspective." *Mens Sana Monogr* 91, no. 1 (2011): 202–9.

Mignolo, Walter. *The Darker Side of Western Modernity: Global Futures, Decolonial Options.* Durham and London: Duke University Press, 2011.

Morales, Aurora Levins. *Medicine Stories: Essays for Radicals.* Durham and London: Duke University Press, 2019.

Nandy, Ashis. *The Intimate Enemy: Loss and Recovery of Self under Colonialism.* New York: Oxford University Press, 1983 [2009].

Rezaire, Tabita. "Decolonial Healing*: In Defense of Spiritual Technologies." In *Art as Social Practice Technologies for Change*, edited by xtine Burrough and Judy Walgren, 151–71. New York: Routledge, 2022.

Rothschild, Babette. *The Body Remembers: The Psychophysiology of Trauma and Trauma Treatment.* New York: W.W. Norton, 2000.

Ryle, Gilbert. *The Concept of Mind.* New York: Barnes and Noble, 1949.

Tuck, Eve. "Suspending Damage: A Letter to Communities." *Harvard Educational Review* 79, no. 3 (2009): 309–427.

Ureña, Carolyn. "Decolonial Embodiment: Fanon, the Clinical Encounter, and the Colonial Wound." *Disability and the Global South* 6, no. 1 (2019): 1640–58.

Van der Kolk, Bessel. "The Body Keeps the Score: Memory and the Evolving Psychobiology of Posttraumatic Stress." *Harvard Review of Psychiatry* 1, no. 5 (1994): 253–65.

Varma, Saiba. "Beyond PTSD: Politics of Visibility in a Kashmiri Clinic." In *Traumatic Pasts in Asia: History, Psychiatry and Trauma from the 1930s to the Present*, edited by Mark Micale and Hans Pols, 268–88. Berghahn Books: New York and Oxford, 2021.

Vora, Kalindi. *Life Support: Biocapital and the New History of Outsourced Labor*. Minneapolis: University of Minnesota Press, 2015.

Walsh, Catherine E. *Rising Up, Living On: Re-Existences, Sowings and Decolonial Cracks*. Durham and London: Duke University Press, 2023.

Whitehead, Gregory. "Display Wounds: Ruminations of a Vulnerologist." In *When Pain Strikes*, edited by Bill Burns, Cathy Busby, and Kim Sawchuk, 133–40. Minneapolis and London: University of Minnesota Press, 1999.

Zaragocin, Sofia, and Martina Angela Caretta. "Cuerpo-Territorio: A Decolonial Feminist Geographical Method for the Study of Embodiment." *Annals of the American Association of Geographers* 111, no. 5 (2019): 1503–18.

Zibechi, Raúl. *Territorios en Resistencia: Cartografía Política de las Periferias Urbanas LatinoAmericanas*. Spain: Zambra Baladre, 2008.

Part I

DECOLONIZING RESEARCH

Figure 1 *Kali (tongues)* by Bhasha Chakrabarti (2016–20).

Chapter 1

COMPLEX CONNECTIONS: COLONIALITY, EMBODIMENT, AND CHILDREN OF COLOR IN THE ARCHIVES

Isabelle Higgins

Introduction: Bodies Recognizing Bodies

In September 2022, after a six-month research fellowship at the Library of Congress, I sent an email to a staff member at the institution with the subject heading, "Representations of Children of Color in Library Archives." I began the email with niceties, before outlining my PhD research project and some of my findings. I have copied two sections of this email below:

> *My research focuses on the adoption of children of color by white American families and as part of my work, I've been seeking to historicize these practices. This means searching for photographs or other representations (written material, prints) that were created with the aim of displaying children of color to make financial profit. I've focused on material created during the period 1860s–1920s. In doing this work, a second set of questions have arisen about the ways in which these documents are archived, and it is primarily this second set of questions that I'm emailing you about now. […]*
>
> *While conducting in-person research in the stereograph collection that is freely available to any researcher […], I came across a number of photographs of naked Black children that were taken for stereograph cards and then sold as entertainment. These included a photograph captioned "Columbia's New Helpers," containing three completely naked Black children under 10 years old facing both towards and away from the camera, holding the hands of a white woman dressed in an American flag. A second set of stereograph cards contains the rhyme "10 little N* Boys"; each photograph of the series shows a group of elementary school aged boys in Jamaica acting out scenes in which they hurt each other, and in some of these they are completely unclothed. I also found images of white children bathing, although in these photographs nudity is a) more partial and b) captured in household scenes as opposed to staged positions of clear subordination.*

I ended the email by asking for further discussion and consideration to be given to how such images are archived in the library. As I awaited a reply, I reflected on how this experience surfaced a central question and tension about how we, as researchers, working in the present, recognize and treat representations of bodies from the past.

To answer this question, I situate my research within a context of coloniality—a global system of intersectionally racialized oppression that continues into the present despite the abolition of many "formal" colonial systems of domination. This is an understanding of our present social context in which "coloniality" and "modernity" are co-constituting realities (Quijano 2007), affecting all aspects of our social, material, and political experiences on both a macro and a micro scale. I draw particularly on the work of Maldonado-Torres (2007), who explains that coloniality may have been established in the context of formal-legal structures, but that the same systems of power continue in a variety of institutions, activities, *and* in our everyday, embodied experiences. How we become aware of and choose to engage with the complexity of these structural relations of power is complex. In the email excerpt, for example, I sought to describe the bodies of the children that I research, but I did not describe the effect that this research had on my body. Yet my bodily response when I found these photographs shaped my actions, including the email I chose to write. This affective response is one that emerges from and relates to a longer history of coloniality too—as Sara Ahmed (2004: 126) reminds us, "histories that stick" shape the body's affective responses to people, places, and things.

So, in this chapter, I attend to the knowledge and the pain inscribed in my body by colonial relations of power and explore how this shaped the research I chose to do. I grapple with my positionality as a researcher, with academic training, which means that "institutionally, our bodies are disciplined to hold and claim certain statuses" (McGranahan et al. 2016), while also reflecting upon how my body as a mixed-race, white-passing White British and Afro-Caribbean woman, shaped my affective responses to my archival research. I work with understandings of embodiment and coloniality that are not fixed, instead orienting myself to what Howse (2019: 202) describes as a "vigilant epistemology," a "critical consciousness [that] is not static, rather it is a constant work in progress which as teachers, researchers and 'producers of knowledge' we have responsibility to maintain." Taking such an approach has led me to conclude that, to challenge the colonial matrix of power, it is fundamental to consider the connections between our bodies and the bodies of those we research in their complexity and contradiction. To achieve this, I turn first to why I was searching for images of children of color in the archive. I then reflect upon stages of the (re)search process chronologically.

Applying: *The Violence of Re(search)*

My PhD research (see Higgins 2023) focuses on how internet use is shaping transnational and transracial adoption in the United States. It has involved digital ethnography and critical techno-cultural discourse analysis (Brock 2018) to explore how intersectional inequalities are reproduced digitally. At the center of the project are a group of children of color whose personal information is shared online by adoption agencies, governments, and adoptive parents who build careers by digitally monetizing the racial alterity of their adopted children.

To understand these processes, I draw on critical race theory, decolonial theory, and "intersectionality as critical social theory" (Collins 2019). My work focuses particularly on the anti-Black racism that constructs and cements the material and embodied realities of these children's lives, as well as the lives of their birth parents. As I have highlighted in previous writing (Higgins, 2023), adults adopting children counted as "special needs" were offered a $6000 tax break after the passing of legislation in 1996. Under this legislation, Black children were included within the "special needs" category *on the basis of* their racial identity (Ortiz and Briggs, 2003). My research has found that today, the categorization of children in state foster care as "special needs" or "hard to place" still includes racial identity and that the placement of a child by state and federal government into this category means that personal data (including photographs, first names, descriptions of disabilities, and in some cases information about whether a child has been sexually abused) is shared by government-funded agencies in the public domain (Higgins 2023). In my broader work, I argue that there is an urgent need to conduct further research and influence policy in this area so that some of the most vulnerable and marginalized children in the United States are not rendered "hypervisible" (Benjamin 2019) in digital spaces.

As my approach to sociological analysis seeks to elucidate how coloniality shapes social relations, I wanted to find historical precedent for the digital practices I had observed. Therefore, I applied for and took up a research fellowship at the Library of Congress in order to try and historicize my digital findings. My decision to focus on the 1860s–1920s was a result of a range of factors, including the ease with which I could access relevant material in library collections and arguments made by social theorists that draw connections (see Daniels 2018, for example) between that time period and our current moment. At the Library of Congress, I thought I would construct a "history of the present" (Hartman 2008) by examining representations of Black children monetized for audiences characterized by whiteness. I believed this research would help me argue that there are real parallels between these non-digital practices and the ways in which white women with Black children monetize their children's racial alterity on YouTube, Instagram, and TikTok today. Thus, using Stuart Hall's (1997) theories on "regimes of representation" and the work of race critical code scholars that place internet practices into a context of racialized oppression (see Brock 2018; Noble 2018; Amaro 2019), I sought to identify and highlight the connections between chattel enslavement, settler colonialism, and a present-day digital global context.

My commitment to exploring the connections between the past and present is long-standing, not only in my research activities but also in my everyday embodied experiences and understandings of the world. Prior to academia, I worked in the campaigns and policy sector in the UK, focusing on projects that foregrounded the realities for children experiencing multiple forms of marginalization, including sexual abuse and gender based violence. During my PhD, I completed a qualification in youth work practice, learning about relational ways of working with children and young people. Beyond my PhD, I hope to develop projects that seek to engage with, and directly benefit, children who are rendered most marginal in our current global system. Not only do I see real academic value and potential in this project to contribute to racial justice, digital justice, and reproductive justice movements, but this approach to research and practice also speaks to and emerges from my own experiences as a mixed-race white British and Afro-Caribbean woman.

I grew up in a low-income, state-benefit-reliant, single-parent household in a rural area of the UK, raised by my mother, who is mixed-race, and my grandmother, who is Black. My childhood was shaped by active othering and racism on a daily basis from people in our geographical proximity, as well as the generational knowledge passed down by my grandmother and great Uncle, who spoke at length about their early life and the life of their parents under colonial rule in Barbados. I have since conducted oral history work with my family, tracing the experiences of my ancestors back to the last two generations who were born into enslavement, learning how the physical features ascribed to these mixed-race babies at birth shaped their treatment on the plantation setting in which they were born and enslaved. When reflecting on these aspects of my experience, I understand that there is a thread that runs throughout my work which attends to how the bodies of children are perceived by others and how that othering shapes their embodied and material experiences of the world.

When applying to the library for my research fellowship, however, I did not speak to all of these realities. I instead argued that I would find real value in placing the digital practices I studied in the context of their emergence. This was indeed the case—the material I found in the library helped me argue that racialized representations of children in the service of whiteness have a long history. What I was not expecting, however, was the way in which my time at the library would be fundamentally shaped by a second reality: much of my six-month fellowship was spent grappling with how such representations of children were archived and cared for. This was because the archival practices I observed were reproducing coloniality in library spaces. The depth and complexity of these processes were not clear when I first arrived at the library, but from the beginning of the fellowship, I was struck by the histories the library contained. I realized quickly that my fellowship would become an ethnographic and autoethnographic, as well as an archival, research experience.

Arriving/Archiving: *Practices of Categorization*

Arriving at the library, I was struck by how the built environment, particularly it's architecture and design, reflected and reproduced colonial relations of power. The walls inside the library's main reading rooms, for example, contain extensive painted depictions of "great men." Carved heads, which are sculptures designed

its | it's|

to represent "the races of the world," look out on Capitol Hill from the Jefferson Building's upper floors, framing the archives that the library building contains. These two examples alone reflect the reinscription of "race" as a fixed category and the connections created between whiteness, patriarchy, and the boundaries of academic knowledge production. Here, I engage with the library ethnographically, embracing what Stoler (2002: 93) refers to as a "move from archive as source to archive as subject." This means I engaged with the built environment *of* the Library of Congress and the archives it contains as an object of study. This was not necessarily my intention ahead of my fellowship, but on my first day at the library, while being shown the paintings of "the great men" and grappling with the existence of the "races of the world" on the walls, I knew that an active, critical, and reflexive engagement with library spaces was already a part of my project.

The desire to critically orient myself toward the archive intensified when I began searching for representations of children of color monetized for mass audiences characterized by whiteness. From the beginning of the project, I was reminded over and over that the archives themselves reflected biases toward colonial modes of collecting, organizing, and categorizing, and that these categorization processes privileged specific and situational understandings of the social world. It proved difficult, for example, to find images of children of color, as this piece of autoethnography describes:

> *I am told by a librarian that I need to use 'creative search terms' to find photographs of children of color in the [...] archive. It takes me five days to realize that I need to search for racial slurs. If I search for 'children' all the 'children' are white. I search for the term 'alligator bait' and find a photograph, taken in the late 1800s, of three small black heads above water. Above them; white men stand on a jetty. 'Alligator bait diving for pennies in Florida' says the caption on the photograph. The entry into the digital archive is identically written.*

In this example, we can see how racialized relations of power are reinscribed in the library's archives in the present. These relations are not only textual— reflected in how archival material is captioned and labeled, for example—but are also shaped by wider archival practices. Children of color were not included as "children" when the archive was designed, and it has not yet been updated to include them. Thus, the power to categorize and organize is exercised by bodies in the present, shaping the visibility and value afforded to bodies affected by racialized marginalization in the past. In the photograph captioned "alligator bait," this representation, as far as I can tell, documents the violently racialized process in which Black children were induced to swim, in water potentially containing alligators, for the amusement of white men. The vulnerability of the bodies in this process and the racially dehumanized nature of their realities are only compounded by the violence involved in photographing them in the water.

This photograph was then made into a stereograph card, and it was this card that I viewed in the archive. These products—small pieces of card upon which photographs were printed—were a booming industry during the late 1800s, produced by a range of photographic companies on a mass scale. Using a stereograph viewer, a small pair of glasses, with each lens trained on a scene photographed from slightly different angles, the images on the card appeared 3D for the viewer. At the time, these were a common source of after-dinner entertainment in white, middle-class homes and were also used as an educational resource in classrooms. When looking at the photograph of the Black heads above water, I found myself horror-struck by the violence involved in rendering this dangerous bodily experience into a commodity that was sold as a source of amusement for audiences characterized by whiteness. I then felt anger at the re-inscriptive violence occurring through the archival practices of cataloging and storing these images by using the caption on the stereograph card as the archival label—racially violent phrases thus found an uncritical home in the archive, and searching for such phrases was the only way that such images could be found. Archival practice, therefore, meant that many Black children were only findable if they were searched for through racial slurs. I grappled, too, with my own bodily responses, knowing that I had to research and use racially violent phrases that had been perhaps used against ancestral members of my own family and community, in order to find the images I needed. Reading about "alligator bait" as a phrase, and its likely etymology, left me shaking.

Searching *for "Children": The Realities of Non-Indexicality*

Because children of color were not afforded indexicality in library spaces, I looked to other historical sources to understand the representational economies prevalent in the United States in the late 1800s and early 1900s. This effort, to locate children who were not recognized as children because of the way they were racialized by the archive, was moved forward hugely by my research into the "World's Fairs." The Columbian Exposition in 1893, the Paris Exposition in 1900, and the Saint Louis "World's Fair" in 1904 were huge events in which hundreds of thousands of people gathered to look at "the wonders of the world" (Reed 2021). The buildings in which these fairs took place were often built especially for this purpose, with state and federal funding accessed and mobilized. Guards were hired to work at the fairs: protecting "the wonders" from the hundreds of thousands of attendees (Reed 2021), who paid entrance fees to look at exhibits, including colonized peoples placed on display (Go 2013).

Thinking about the "World's Fair" as material environments, purpose built as sites for embodied experience, also served a second purpose: it allowed me to place the built environment of the Library of Congress in a wider contextual frame. The Thomas Jefferson Building, where I worked, for example, was opened in 1900. I therefore deepened my historical understanding of the turn of the twentieth century, recognizing that, in a range of ways, US government actors cemented their colonial dominance by creating a collection of built environments that were all concerned with categorization, organization, and display. Within the library, many of the first images I found in which children of color were in fact taken at the "World's Fair." In preliminary research, I located photographs of Filipino and

North American indigenous peoples (both adults and children), photographed while they were placed on display at the St Louis "World's Fair," quite literally being watched by a majority white, US audience. The display of the bodies of these children of color was a recursive, intertextual, multi-layered process. Not only were children placed on display in the "World's Fair," but their images were captured and became products in themselves as stereograph cards.

Finding these stereograph cards led me to search the stereograph collection more broadly for other representational economies taking place in the late 1800s, and it was through this searching that I learned about vaudeville performance— popular touring shows made up of short dance, comedy, and acting performances (Davis et al. 2005). Searching through historic records of vaudeville shows, filtering for the racially derogatory word "pickaninnies," I pulled together a list of white women performers who used Black child performers in their shows. Searching for these women's names with the word "pickannines" in the library's digital prints and photograph's archive returned many results of Black children photographed as backing performers for white women actresses and singers. In these photographs, the children were sometimes unclothed, sometimes singing, dancing, and playing instruments. I searched for information about these children—their names, their histories, their lives after their performance, but it was exceedingly hard, if not impossible in nearly every case, to trace them. In a similar way, children photographed at the "World's Fair" were often captioned with the name "Columbia"—a form of dehumanization which rendered such children untraceable today.

Hartman (2008) writes about the difficulties of imagining, speculating about, caring for, and representing those who are racially dehumanized in life, death, and in the archive, where only fragments of their lives are recorded. She explains that "the loss of stories sharpens the hunger for them. So it is tempting to fill in the gaps and to provide closure where there is none" (Hartman 2008: 8). Looking at these photographs, at the eyes of these children placed on display or on stage, I grappled with this tension, and with the realities of these children's embodied experiences. My imagining of their realities was complicated by the fact that nearly all of the photographs I looked at were staged. I therefore found myself considering the racialized violence of a representational economy in which children of color were directed to pose for a camera, with the images of their bodies recast as products to be sold on the open market. By thinking about these contexts of production, I returned again and again to the fact that photographs I examined were reminders of the visible and violent articulations of racialization and colonization. People were moved across geographical space in order for their bodies to be looked at. Similar experiences are examined by Mitchell (1991) who describes the experience of Egyptian delegates at the 1900 Paris exposition, who realized the exposition was a space in which "one was liable to become an object on exhibit" for others in attendance (Mitchell 1991: 5).

Thinking about the images of children in this social and historical context, I considered how the experience of being placed on display and/or photographed might have affected their embodied experience, subjective self-understanding, and their understanding of the world around them. It also led me to consider the people who made up the audience: what did it mean to objectify others quite literally and actively, gazing at their bodies in a "living ethnological exhibit"? (Go 2013) or on a stereograph card as a form of entertainment? Frankenberg (1993: 17) explains that "[w]hile discursively generating and marking a range of cultural and racial Others as different from an apparently stable Western or white self, the Western self is itself produced *as an effect* of the Western discursive production of its other." The experience of being looked at and the act of looking are fundamentally codependent processes. And this co-constitution of self and other is an *embodied* process, in which the subjectivity of different actors was produced and reproduced through the placement of certain bodies in certain places. Yet I cannot know how it felt to be these children, placed on display, or how it felt to be the audience, looking at them. And, as Hartman (2008) reminds us, these limits to what can be known are shaped by the racialized violence enacted *through* the archives—in what material is stored, and how and why. But I too have looked at these representations of these children's bodies—my subjectivity is not exempt from these processes of looking. Both my ability to look and the effect of looking were shaped by my positionality and embodied realities in the archives.

Looking *at Photographs of Children: The Pain of Embodied Experience*

I turn now to examine the moment in which I found the images that I describe at the beginning of this chapter. This moment marks a movement from my searching of the library's digitized archive to in-person research in the stereograph collection. It is also a productive moment to consider how my own embodied experience shaped the research process. In my email at the start of the chapter, I state that I "came across" the images I describe—this is because the images were not stored in the "children" section, but instead placed in the "miscellaneous" category of the stereograph collection—which consisted of rows of filing cabinets in the library's Prints & Photographs division. I searched physical index cards for the correct cabinets and file dividers within the cabinets, learning quickly that the indexical word "children" led me almost exclusively to children who were white. A librarian advised me to look under different ethnicity labels for the subcategory of "children," and this led me toward some images. Here, I found the image of the three naked Black children. I also flicked through the index cards, unprompted, to the "miscellaneous" category. Under this category, I found the heading "racial caricature" and under this was the '10 little N* boys' set of cards that I also describe in my email.

When I found these images, I left the library to call my brother, upset with both the violence contained within the photographs and the violence enacted by how they were organized within the library collections. Our conversation jumped forward and back: we talked about how my findings connected to our collective familial experiences, and we discussed, from a professional standpoint, whether it was reasonable or ethical for me to photograph the representations I had found, because they contained child nudity. We also discussed, as we usually do, how my white-passing body, and his visibly mixed-race body, shape the social research and active youth work that employs us. In that moment, contained within my body, was the conflicting emotional desire to connect my research to my own history and positionality, while also considering the ethical implications related to finding these representations of children's bodies.

I thought, for example, about the realities of growing up in a state benefit-reliant household—a reality I connect to the economic positioning of the Windrush generation of Afro-Caribbean migrants to the UK and the subsequent experiences of my grandmother and mother. I remember standing in lines for hours in a welfare center in the UK in the 1990s, knowing that the paperwork we needed to receive our payments might have been lost, but was eventually found stored in the "other" section of a governmental bureaucratic system. I felt it was this memory contained in my body that led me to look under the "miscellaneous" heading in the stereograph's archive. Yet I also knew that my access to these archives was shaped by the privilege I hold: I am a PhD student at the University of Cambridge, who, during this research project, lived in Washington DC and carried out research at the Library of Congress funded by the UK government. In addition, my identity as a white-passing person shapes my research: the opportunities I have been afforded have been shaped by my proximity to whiteness, and the way in which my body can move, often unnoticed, within built environments characterized by whiteness. Leaving the library to call my brother relied upon my physical movement through security scanners and past the eyes of Capitol policemen. The way my body tends to be read by others often leads to ease of access through these spaces in which racialized regimes of governmentality and violence are expressed.

Analyzing this moment through the lens of decolonial theory, I am struck by Maldonado-Torres (2007) attention to the range of avenues through which coloniality is (re)produced. He explains that in academic culture, how we think about ourselves, engage with others, and in countless other ways too, coloniality is felt and experienced, continuing to shape and structure everyday life. Attention to academic performance and epistemological structures has been explored by a number of decolonial thinkers (see Quijano 2007; Megjhi 2020) who engage with the "coloniality of knowledge"—the ways in which coloniality draws boundaries around what we think we can know and how we know it. Sometimes, however, I think that attention to epistemes can risk foreclosing discussions of how "knowledge," though often abstractedly conceptualized, shapes our immediate experience, placement, bodily and affective responses. Rizvi (2016) states:

> Our ability to understand ourselves in relation to everything else is predicated upon the ability to understand and contextualize the real, tangible, sensory aspect of moving through the world as compared to conceptual, abstract notions of thinking of our bodies in the world.

Consider the moment I found the photographs. Often, I find myself returning to the maxim that "our bodies are a source of social knowledge"—that is, what we feel can teach us about the social world, even if we are not able to linguistically conceptualize or capture our feelings. What did my body tell me then, when I found these images? I felt a tightness in my chest, a spasm in my belly, a constriction of my throat, and a desperate sense to move, as quickly as possible, away from where I was. It was after honoring this and moving out of the library (a space where spoken conversation itself is prohibited) that I found myself calling my brother. Without that set of unconscious, embodied activities, I am not sure I would be exploring these questions in this writing. We could interpret these embodied experiences using many lenses and languages, but I want to draw attention to their existence and power. *The emergence of the feelings within my body happened as a result of my particular body being in a specific place at a specific time.* And my embodied experiences shaped the knowledge that I am now producing. If we follow this line of thought further, we see that this embodied knowledge is now being translated into a written chapter that will exist within a book that will find one home on the shelves of the Library of Congress in Washington, DC—the same place where this research began.

Writing *about Children: The Complexities of Representation*

In response to the images I found, I wrote. This writing has taken many different forms, but in each, I grappled with a set of contradictions: the children whom I found myself studying were no longer alive, and their representations were not offered the care and attention which I believed they deserved. Here, I found myself coming up against a limit in my reading of decolonial theory. Maldonado-Torres (2007: 262), for example, explains that:

> The decolonial attitude [...] demands responsibility and the willingness to take many perspectives, particularly the perspectives and points of view of those whose very existence is questioned and produced as insignificant.

Throughout my research, the difficulty of foregrounding the perspectives and points of view of the children whose bodies I have looked at in the archives struck me repeatedly. Nearly all of these children are unnamed in the stereograph photographic captions and thus proved truly untraceable during my research time. Over and over, when trying to trace the children whose bodies I had studied, I recognized the true power of racialized dehumanization processes—images of their bodies were created as objects to be consumed, rendering the realities of their lives invisible. I therefore struggled with Maldonado-Torres's (2007: 262) urge that decolonial thinkers pay attention to "the perspectives and points of view of those whose very existence is questioned and produced as insignificant." How is it possible to pay attention to the perspectives and points of view of a group of children, who are not even categorized as "children" within the library archive system today? Children who were photographed, always unnamed and sometimes unclothed, their bodies rendered as objects to be consumed within a colonial system of domination?

Herein lies a crucial paradox: I too am speaking (or writing) about these children, placing my body in relation to theirs. And this research paradox also emerges from a history and context of coloniality. Julian Go (2013), for example, draws attention to the fact that the first Congress on Social Sciences was held alongside the St Louis "World's Fair." This example reminds us that some academic disciplines were institutionalized as socially legitimated types of knowledge production in a context in which people of color were literally moved from their homes and their families to be gazed at by majority white audiences. Our disciplines occurred in relation to these contexts and are shaped by the embodied experiences of social scientists living in these contexts. Now, roughly 120 years after the "World's Fair," I am building my career in relation to the bodies of the children who were photographed and placed on display. How much change has there been in the disciplinary relationships implicated here? As a sociologist, I am still creating knowledge reliant on the existence of these children and the nonconsensual representation of their bodies. And yet, returning to Maldonado-Torres's (2007) provocation, my research has convinced me of the importance of rendering visible the ways in which systemic colonial relations of power have shaped, and continue to shape, the treatment of children of color's bodies.

Writing, for me, has been a method through which I can make some of these relations of power visible and trace the complex, connected ways in which coloniality is expressed in everyday practice. During my time at the Library, I wrote the following piece of autoethnography about the photographs I've described in this chapter:

> *I look at these photographs and my heart hurts. The stories behind these photographs are incomplete, unknown. But I will tell the stories I have and try to explain why I think they're important. First of all though, it's worth thinking about the violence that this telling might do. These are not children I know, they are not children who (as far as I know) I am related to. The lives of these children when they were no longer children is unknown. All of them had parents, some of them may have had siblings, some might have gone on to have children of their own. I think about what these children's children might think if they knew I was writing and thinking about their ancestors. What does it mean that if I share photographs of these ancestors, who, as much as their personhood may have been denied, were people with relationalities, subjectivities and preferences, senses of humor, likes and dislikes, favorite seasons, favorite foods, favorite people. How do I talk about these children without 'flattening' them to the oppression they experienced? And does this 'flattening' matter? I think it does—because it is what I am arguing against. I am claiming that the representations of these children flatten them to objects engaged with by an audience characterized by whiteness. It is this 'flattening', this dehumanization, which may have justified the ways in which these children, and countless others like them, were (mis)treated by others. And as an adult, who was once a child who experienced racialised (mis)treatment from others, I cannot write and think about these children without my heart hurting. What was behind their smiles?*

This piece of autoethnography speaks to the power relations implicated in my research project (see also Arani, this volume). There is a marked movement from this initial piece of writing to my writing now, nine months later. I do not display any photographs of children in this chapter, not wishing to show the placement of their bodies without their consent—given that their consent will always be impossible to receive. I have grappled with the difficulties of describing their embodied experiences, aided by Hartman's (2008: 12) recognition of the "productive tension" involved in conveying anti-Black violence alongside the "inevitable failure of any attempt to represent." I have grappled more broadly with my role as a researcher and writer, reminded by Smith (2012: 226) that, as researchers, we "must get the story right as well as tell the story well." I cannot tell these children's stories. But I can tell my account of searching for their representations and finding them.

In so doing, I hope to have shown how coloniality is re-expressed in the present. The power relations implicated here have shaped my desire to search, my ability to search, the ease with which I've searched, my embodied and affective responses to searching, and my writing about this process. They've shaped the placement of the children's bodies, their photographing, their commodification, their storage, and the ease with which they can be found. In her "Black Living Data Booklet," Day (2020) argues for "data stewardship" when digital data about Black lives is created and engaged with. Though I have focused on archival data, only some of which is digitized, I think this notion of "stewardship" is useful and productive for data of all types. How can we, as writers and researchers, encourage and enact appropriate "stewardship" over the data we engage with? And what does it mean, returning to Howse (2019), with whom I opened this chapter, to be "vigilant" about our stewardship?

In this case, my stewardship has involved writing as a method. I have written for myself (to help me understand the feelings in my body and the questions I have about my work), written to the library (to try and change the way in which representations of children of color are cared for), and written this chapter (to share my research process in the hope it might be productive for others). All three of these writing processes are connected because, in each of them, I have reflected on how my engagement with the representations of children of color might reproduce or challenge colonial relations of power. Through this process, I have come to understand my research as an always-unfinished project that contains tensions, engages with contradictions, and makes connections between different aspects of human social life in both the present and the past. My hope is that by clearly elucidating and highlighting these connections between everyday, embodied experiences and a wider structural context of coloniality, we might move closer to dismantling them.

Bibliography

Ahmed, Sara. "Collective Feelings: Or, the Impressions Left by Others." *Theory, Culture & Society* 21, no. 2 (2004): 25–42.

Amaro, Ramon. *As If.* [online] E-flux.com. 2019. https://www.e-flux.com/architecture/becoming-digital/248073/as-if/ (accessed August 16, 2020).

Benjamin, Ruha. *Race after Technology: Abolitionist Tools for the New Jim Code*. Medford: Polity Press, 2019.

Brock, Andre. "Critical Technocultural Discourse Analysis." *New Media & Society* 20, no. 3 (2018): 1012–30.

Collins, Patricia Hill. *Intersec@onality as Cri@cal Social Theory*. Durham, NC: Duke University Press, 2019.

Daniels, Jessie. "The Algorithmic Rise of the 'Alt-Right.'" *Contexts* 17, no. 1 (2018): 60–5.

Davis, Jacquelien Z., Barbara G. Fleischman, and Lawrence A. Fleischman. *Vaudeville Nation, NYPL, Vaudeville Nation*. 2005. http://webstatic.nypl.org/exhibitions/vaudeville/credits.html (accessed May 4, 2023).

Day, Faithe. "Black Living Data Booklet." 2020. https://static1.squarespace.com/static/5f402e034b33c773cedbd428/t/5f5578b66699dc5f7fd72ef6/1599437000245/THE±BLD±Booklet±%284%29.pdf (accessed May 4, 2023).

Frankenberg, Ruth. *White Women, Race Matters: The Social Construction of Whiteness*. Minneapolis: University of Minnesota Press, 1993.

Go, Julian. "The Emergence of American Sociology in the Context of Empire." In *Sociology & Empire: The Imperial Entanglements of a Discipline*, edited by George Steinmetz, 83–103. Durham, NC: Duke University Press, 2013.

Hall, Stuart. *Representation: Cultural Representations and Signifying Practices / Edited by Stuart Hall*. London: Sage in association with the Open University, 1997.

Hartman, Saidiya. "Venus in Two Acts." *Small Axe: A Journal of Criticism* 12, no. 2 (2008): 1–14.

Higgins, Isabelle. "Classified Children: A Critical Analysis of the Digital Interfaces and Representations that Mediate Adoption in the United States." *New Media & Society* (2023): 1–18. https://doi.org/10.1177/14614448231156852.

Howse, Melody. "Creating a Space within the German Academy." In *To Exist Is to Resist: Black Feminism in Europe*, edited by Akwugo Emejulu and Francesca Sobande. London: Pluto Press, 2019.

Maldonado-Torres, Nelson. "On the Coloniality of Being." *Cultural Studies* 21, no. 2–3 (2007): 240–70.

McGranahan, Carole, Kaifa Roland, and Bianca C. Williams. "Decolonizing Anthropology: A Conversation with Faye V. Harrison, Part I." *Savage Minds*, 2016.

Meghji, Ali. "Introduction: Sociology in the Metropole." In *Decolonizing Sociology: An Introduction*. Cambridge and Medford, MA: Polity Press, 2020. https://savageminds.org/2016/05/02/decolonizing-anthropology-a-conversation-with-faye-v-harrison-part-i/ (accessed June 3, 2023).

Mitchell, Timothy. *Colonising Egypt*. Berkeley: University of California Press, 1991.

Noble, Safiya Umoja. *Algorithms of Oppression: How Search Engines Reinforce Racism*. New York: New York University Press, 2018.

Ortiz, Ana Teresa, and Laura Briggs. "The Culture of Poverty, Crack Babies, and Welfare Cheats: The Making of the 'Healthy White Baby Crisis.'" *Social Text* 21, no. 3(76) (2003): 39–57.

Quijano, Aníbal. "Coloniality and Modernity/Rationality." *Cultural Studies* 21, no. 2–3 (2007): 168–78.

Reed, Christopher. "The Black Presence at the World's Columbian Exposition, 1893." *Oxford African American Studies Center*. 2021. Retrieved March 3, 2023. https://oxfordaasc.com/view/10.1093/acref/9780195301731.001.0001/acref-9780195301731-e-78818.

Rizvi, Uzma Z. "Decolonization as Care." In *Slow Reader: A Resource for Design Thinking and Practice*, edited by Carolyn F. Strauss and Ana Paula Pais, 85–95. Amsterdam: Valiz, 2016.

Smith, Linda Tuhiwai. *Decolonizing Methodologies: Research and Indigenous Peoples.* Second ed. London: Zed books, 2012.

Stoler, Ann Laura. "Colonial Archives and the Arts of Governance." *Archival Science* 2, no. 1–2 (2002): 87–109.

Chapter 2

BURNOUT: A QUEER FEMME OF COLOR AUTO-ETHNOGRAPHY

Alexia Arani

In the years before Covid-19 hit the United States, like many queer femmes of color who are care workers, organizers, and activists, I was already not okay. I was living in San Diego, beginning dissertation fieldwork, juggling multiple organizing responsibilities for local queer and trans communities, doing a disproportionate amount of reproductive labor for my household, and grappling with the ongoing, cumulative effects of living with grief, PTSD, depression, and anxiety—medicalized categories for embodied states of intensity that I had, for the most part, folded into myself and normalized. Living under Trump's presidency, there was a palpable sense of precarity in our heavily militarized border city, where many queer and trans folks struggled to maintain housing, healthcare, and employment. Living on occupied lands, stolen first from the Kumeyaay people and later from the state of Mexico, the urgent and sorely needed care work of collective survival was marked by inequity and social abandonment. There were far too few of us picking up the pieces.

I spent most of my graduate school experience—roughly 2014–20—immersed in the endless labor of organizing mutual aid efforts and materially and emotionally supporting people in my broader queer/trans of color community. At the same time that I was researching the psychic impacts of colonization, racial capitalism, and cisheteropatriarchy on multiply marginalized communities, I was myself—a multiply marginalized person—struggling with the effects of colonization, racial capitalism, and cisheteropatriachy on my own queer femme of color bodymind. Under colonialist logics of extraction, I felt I had to prove my value through my labor—to the academy, my communities, my household and partnerships. Oft-neoliberalized discourses of privilege led me to believe that, as a light-skinned, mixed-race person with access to family wealth, rest was a luxury I had an ethical obligation to forego. Surviving under these conditions often required a disconnect from my bodymind and spirit.

Through the ups and downs of stressors and psychic states, I predominantly made sense of my (dis)embodied experiences using the framework of burnout.

My journal entries in this era repeat: *I'm feeling burnt out today, I'm getting close to burnout, I've been burnt out recently*. While the language of burnout has existed since at least the 1970s (Freudenberger 1974; Maslach 1976), it has taken newfound salience since the 2016 election, with a slew of thinkpieces and op-eds proclaiming millennials like me "the burnout generation" (Peterson 2019). It made sense that burnout—broadly conceived as a symptom of overwork, exhaustion, and alienation in capitalist societies—would be the language I (and many other queer femmes of color) oriented toward to make sense of our experiences.

However, as I tracked my experiences of burnout ethnographically, and sat with the burnout narratives I collected from other queer femme of color care workers, I began to recognize that my own—that our—femme of color lived experiences exceeded hegemonic burnout discourses. My positionality—as a queer femme of color survivor of suicide loss, who has coped with trauma and grief by funneling care into precarious queer and trans communities—made the whitewashed story of the American Dream thwarted by exploitative gig labor hardly relevant for me. The wounds my communities and I were navigating were not newly forged but were inherited across generations. Our burnout was not the result of the 2008 economic recession and ensuing efforts to gain financial stability. Ours were wounds of dispossession, diaspora, and the daily struggle to forge a sense of safety and belonging in a place that continually reminds you that you aren't wanted.

Likewise, the dominant models for burnout "recovery," which stress better work/life balance, taking breaks, and pampering oneself did not get to the root of my fundamental wounds. While intermittent camping trips did help me stay afloat, this was a practice of returning to myself, communing with nature, and conjuring a vision of what my life could look like beyond colonialist and capitalist constraints. Returning to my body, and to modes of relationality that affirmed and uplifted my unique humanity, were more important for my self-care than any scented product or structured wellness routine. In other words, my journey was not one of recovery, but of healing. My burnt-out queer femme of color bodymind needed a decommodified and decolonized reorientation to body, relations, and world.

Below, I offer excerpts from my field notes during the first year of my dissertation fieldwork to share the affective experience of living in my traumatized, burnt-out, queer femme of color bodymind. I hope to take you on a journey through the (dis)connections to embodiment, the narrowing and expansion of perspective, and the never-ending labor demands made on queer femme of color caregivers. My positionality as a middle-class and mixed-race person with access to family wealth shapes this burnout narrative in important ways. Poor, working-class, and undocumented workers are arguably the most impacted by burnout yet remain the least studied and represented. While my dissertation delves into the burnout narratives of queer femmes of color who are disproportionately impacted by capitalist disenfranchisement, colonization, and racism (Arani 2022), it is a practice of queer, feminist, and decolonial scholarship—as well as personal healing—for me to tell my own story.

As self-care booms into a massive industry, and the radical politics of rest are appropriated to promote expensive wellness retreats, it is important to not lose sight of coloniality and capitalism as the source of much existential and embodied suffering (Kim and Schalk 2021; Hersey 2022). From extractive logics that promote overworking and self-interested behavior, to weakened networks of social support, to loss of cultural healing practices, coloniality haunts the weary bones of every burnt-out femme of color organizer who wonders why they are so damn tired, day after day. While reading this piece, if you see parts of yourself reflected back in my words, I want you to know: These feelings are not your fault. Your exhaustion is a survival response. Your bodymind needs rest, connection, joy, attunement to embodiment, and spirit. Pharmaceutical medication may save your life (Prozac was a game-changer for me in 2003, and again in 2021) but it will never provide collective liberation. Work every day to extend yourself infinite compassion and grace as you work to reclaim your own trajectory of healing. I see you. I embrace you. You're not alone.

February 5, 2019

I'm going to start tracking burnout ethnographically. I wake up at 8:30 a.m. I brush my hair and teeth, rinse my face, put on the deodorant my partner and I make to avoid poisoning ourselves with aluminum, dab lavender oil on my wrists and neck, and get dressed. I walk to the community healthcare clinic down the street where I sit in on Lana's psychiatry appointment, as part of my research on how queer and trans people of color navigate care. The psychiatrist is an older white man with a stunted affect.

"Depression?" he asks.

"Moderate," Lana responds.

"Anxiety?"

"Manageable."

"Panic attacks?"

"Thankfully none."

The psychiatrist refills her prescriptions. Afterward, we get breakfast. We talk about coming out, her transition, how she manages her medication, and how she's learned to rank the severity of her anxiety and depression for her psychiatry appointments. We talk about her physical tics, and tears form in her eyes as she softly tells me that she wishes they would stop. She wants to experience physical intimacy and doesn't want potential partners to be scared off by her spasms, depression, or anxiety. We are wandering into vulnerable and important territory, over plates of eggs, beans, and rice. A man walks past on the busy city street, shouting about the apocalypse, as I reach out for Lana's hand. She tells me others don't really know her like this; that not a lot of people can hold space to hear about trauma.

I pay for the meal, hug her goodbye, and go next door to a coffee shop to write. I take my time to write out an ethnographic narrative instead of a sterile data dump, which has been my approach to field notes thus far. When I finish, I check why my iCloud isn't updating. I try to log in using different combinations of username and password, but none of my attempts work. I have to reset the password and wait for the link in my inbox, refreshing, refreshing, refreshing. I reset the contact device because it is hooked to my partner's phone, and I begin to back up all my files. When it's done uploading, I send an email I've been putting off for months. Next, I check out the FedEx website to see if I can submit the flyers for the upcoming Love Affair—a queer dance party and mutual aid fundraiser I organize monthly—so I can save time by not having to use the printers in the shop. I have to make an account, then verify my email address, refreshing, refreshing, refreshing. I find out that if I upload the flyers, I can't pick them up until 3:30 p.m.—that's hours away. I decide to walk to FedEx instead, because I'd rather handle the errands now, while I'm out of the house. I email my advisor to see if he will write a letter for a grant application for me. I mark the due date in my planner and add it to my to-do list for mid-month. At 1:15 p.m., I FaceTime with a student who has questions about her exam. I break it down into steps and give her advice on how to approach the readings. She thanks me and tells me she was on the brink of tears because she was feeling so lost and overwhelmed. She works and is currently on break.

I log off after our conversation and walk to the bank to pay rent. I look at my phone while I wait in line. Next, I walk to Whole Foods and pick up vegetable broth, because I am planning dinner as I walk, and remember I need it for risotto. I go to FedEx Office for my prints. Because I don't have a flash drive, I have to email it to them and wait five minutes until they receive it. We do a test print to check the quality and then print nineteen more. I take some tape from their workstation and carefully stick it to the ends of the envelope so it can be reused for flyering. I stop by the coffee shop where I was working earlier and hang up the flier before walking home. At my house, I move the load of laundry I started that morning from wash to dry and see that my dad texted, "Can you talk now?" I decide to get the dogs ready for a walk and call him. I periodically cross the street to avoid other dogs, tugging them along when they want to sniff in opposite directions. My dad called to tell me I need to redo my taxes. I already spent two hours and $80 to use a tax platform that advertised itself as free, so I tell him I'm not going to refile.

He asks how fieldwork is going and if taking a break from teaching is making a difference for my work. I tell him I had an incredibly productive month and there's no way that would have happened if I had been teaching. I tell him I might need to take a step back because I'm doing too much and stretching myself thin. I ask what he's been up to, and he says he's busy. I remind him of the importance of work-life balance, and he lists all the countries he got to visit last year. I'm glad he prioritizes doing what he loves, but I wish his vision of self-care was more sustainable. He tells me another one of his friends died, unexpectedly. He was only sixty-five. I ask if he has rituals to remember them by. I know that every time we enter a Catholic Church, he lights a candle for his mother. He tells me he lights candles for her and many others, as he's sure I can imagine (my sister, and her death, hang in those unspoken words). I'm glad my father has his own practice of memorializing, but I know he only steps into a Catholic Church once or twice a year.

I return home from my walk, say bye to my dad. I notice the dryer door swung open. I close it and restart the load.

I sit.
I feel my body feeling tired.
I feel my lungs feeling strained and prickly, perhaps from being out in the cold.

I read updates on social media. Ten minutes later, I get ready for yoga. I feel tired but need to do this for myself. I see yoga as my "self-care." I leave at 4:12 p.m. and get there a few minutes before 4:30 p.m., setting up in a spot on the side because the man who usually sets up in the middle annoys and distracts me. I lie down to rest before class starts, trying to ignore the fluorescent lights shining in my eyes. I'm restless as the instructor runs through the same thing she says every week. I'm especially agitated when she talks about how we're being selfish for taking this time for ourselves, and how that's okay. I think about how yoga is about selflessness, and how I end every session touching my forehead to the ground and dedicating the benefits of the session to all sentient beings. After the class, a young, thin, white woman loudly says "namaste," smiles, and claps.

I walk home. I prep the squash. I think about showering but don't want to do it. I switch over the laundry and fold and put away clothes instead. Catching myself falling into a bad mood, I decide to smoke pot and take a very hot shower. In the shower, I start to sing—long, slow, droning notes. I shift my weight into each foot, seeing how changing the position changes the sound. I used to sing like this alone in the mountains, sitting on the earth, touching twigs, and watching insects scuttle by. I remind myself to start playing the flute again. Music is important. I need a creative outlet. Walking dogs and cooking dinner are not all I need to decompress, especially when they begin to feel like chores. I get out of the shower, feeling better. I make dinner. Usually, I have music, a podcast, or TV—but I decide to lean into the silence. The risotto takes longer than expected. I remember I need to rebottle my kombucha, but I don't have the energy. I'm thinking about the art show I am organizing on Friday to fundraise for my friend's surgery and worrying it will be a disaster. I don't have the energy or excitement to plan anything special for the event. It feels like a chore I have to take care of, something that just needs to get done.

A friend texts to ask if it's too late to request images to include in the art show. I tell them yes, but I can arrange to get them prints afterward. I ask for help with promotion. They ask if we can have a DJ and other artists sell items during the show. I tell them I support it, but I don't have the capacity to organize it. They say they'll handle it. I feel tired seeing the notifications. In the moments between measuring broth, shredding cheese, and stirring rice, I message a lawyer doing border advocacy work to see when we can have a phone conversation. He suggests tomorrow night. I tell him I might be busy with installation for the art show. I'm also thinking I might be relaxing with my partner Tiana, and our time together is sacred. Another voice tells me Tiana will be understanding if I need to step away.

My partner Dylan finally gets home around 7:00 p.m., after a long day on campus. He still has work to do. I decide to FaceTime Tiana while my risotto bakes. When the food is cooked and Dylan is done studying, I tell Tiana I have to go. I haven't seen or talked to Dylan all day. We smoke, eat the risotto, and watch *The Good Place*. We're both excited about how the new season critiques capitalism. I start to fall asleep on the couch around 10:00 p.m. and decide to get ready for bed. In bed, I receive a text from a drag performer telling me they pushed back the time of the performances so their partner could attend the show. Dylan and I discuss it, annoyed. He tells me he thinks he needs a break from Love Affair. It's too stressful and he's busy with school. I say nothing, but I'm not happy with his response. We are supporting the community and creating a night and space that don't exist. It's important and needed. I think about how we haven't had quality time recently. Dylan is usually in class, doing homework, or working.

I go to sleep and dream of my sister Alaina. She was back among the living, and it upset the natural balance of things. I spill a glass of red wine, and it pours out clear and white. I look up at her, with urgency, reading this as a sign. "You need to go, NOW!" I sense there is something coming for us, that this blending of worlds is not to be permitted, even in the sacred realm of dream space.

When I wake, I have twenty minutes to get ready before class. It is cold, and I want tea, but I didn't get up early enough, so I refill my water bottle and walk to the shuttle. I ride on the bus, in rush hour traffic, for 35 minutes. I sit through an hour of class, working on what I can during the lecture, scribbling notes in my planner. We get out 10 minutes early. I sit in the sun and eat a peanut butter and jelly sandwich, scrolling on my phone. I think idly that I will quickly hit my social media allowance on my phone, though I will probably ignore this limit, and continue scrolling. I walk to the library for office hours. I know nobody is going to show up. I'm still feeling heavy feelings after dreaming about my sister, so I sit down and write about death, dreams, and grief.

With no interruptions, office hours end. I walk to the bus, get on, and walk home. I have an hour before I need to meet Simone. I rebottle my kombucha, pouring from the main container into smaller jars with pieces of peeled and sliced ginger and berries that I left out in the sunshine earlier that morning so they could thaw. When I'm done, I wipe down the counters, sticky and stained blue from berry juice. I'm nauseous but need to eat, so I make myself avocado toast.

Simone messages me that she's running late. I sit and wait. When she's ready, I go pick her up. I always feel overwhelmed driving her around. We have to switch between multiple interstates, so I'm constantly merging and exiting, trying to listen attentively because she usually begins sharing updates before we reach our destination. I have a nice, new car with motion sensors, but today is one of several days that my blind-spot warning doesn't go off, and I realize while I'm changing lanes that I'm too close to another car. I speed up and swerve, panicking that I'm going to hit them.

Amid these highway negotiations, I ask Simone how her unemployment process is going. We talk about the paperwork she has to fill out, how her friend helped her with the forms, and the delays in receiving her first payment. We get to a hipster coffee bar, and I put up a Love Affair poster in the bathroom. I pay for my drink, and hers, and we take a corner seat. We discuss how she's looking for a new therapist again, how sessions she thought would be covered weren't and cost $130 for two appointments. She tells me about her recent depressive episode, how she wasn't leaving the house and was crying all the time. I ask what she does for self-care when this happens. She explains how she tries to take care of herself, but notes the barriers in the medical system, and how it's hard to find friends or community members with whom she can talk openly about mental health. She tells me that people usually don't know how to respond, or that when she tries opening up, the person doesn't ever hang out with her again or make plans to follow up. She tells me she's more comfortable with complete strangers or professionals because then she doesn't have to worry about dumping everything on someone or whether they have the capacity to respond.

I feel my energy draining during the session. I am struggling to remember the details of our conversation. My patience and ability to be present are depleting more rapidly by the second. I ask if we can wrap up. She says yes, and talks more, and then I suggest leaving again, and we get our things. As we leave, we stop by nearby coffee shops so I can put up more flyers. We keep talking as I work. I find myself feeling increasingly overwhelmed and tired. I drop her off. I drive home. Dylan is there when I return. I tell him I'm feeling pretty burnt out. I heat up some leftovers and take a minute to eat them. I sit down on the couch, get out my laptop, and begin to write. Later, I crawl into bed with the dogs. Tiana comes over when they get off work, and they crawl into bed with me. Their tenderness and care make me break down and cry. Being together creates space for me to feel vulnerable and reflect and articulate my feelings—overwhelmed.

February 18, 2019

I haven't been writing much lately. As I wrote on February 6, I felt super burnt out after meeting with Simone. It had been a few weeks in the making. I got to a point where I felt exhausted all the time and dreaded doing anything. I was in a sour mood about the art show I organized. I barely had any capacity to do anything special. Luckily, other people came through that day and helped make it a good event.

I'm finding that when I'm feeling burnt out, I dread my phone. When I see new messages, I don't want to read them because I figure there will be some action expected of me beyond reading the message. I'm finding burnout makes me impatient and short with people I'm trying to organize. When people have ideas or special requests, I get annoyed, because I'm already at capacity.

Last week, I felt really exhausted all the time, with no energy, and feeling sad. I kept wondering why I hadn't bounced back yet. Tiana reminded me that I recently had a meltdown, and it takes time to recover. I purposely tried to schedule myself less last week. I spent a lot of time lying down, allowing myself to be still, and to rest. I spent a lot of time with Dylan and Tiana, ordering in food, being with the dogs, getting high, and watching TV.

I started to feel the burnout lift on Thursday, after therapy. When I mentioned to my therapist that I've been organizing a lot, her eyes widened—"On top of everything else?" When I described my average day, she pointed out that it sounds like a lot, back-to-back. She insisted that I need to *slow down,* find time just to be still, and to try and clear my mind of my constant processing of the day, plans for the future, and organizing.

As an able-bodied person, I'm not sure I get to claim crip knowledge—but I'm thinking about all the crip wisdom I've been learning from Leah Lakshmi Piepzna-Samarasinha: the power in stillness, in resting, in being forced to rest. What an intense world we live in where we need affirmations to convince ourselves that it's okay to rest. It's wild that my research revolves around this social movement toward rest, care, and resilience, and while I understand this on a theoretical level, I still struggle to de-internalize these messages and not measure my worth based on how much I accomplish.

March 21, 2019

I've been feeling heavy-hearted recently and feeling the need to process. I've been tired and antisocial this month. I guess it's the lingering effects of burnout, but it feels weird given that I've really slowed down a lot this month. Though I know that for me, "slowing down" is probably equivalent to other people's normal. It's hard not to compare yourself to others doing the most (single mothers doing fieldwork while teaching multiple classes) and feeling like what I'm doing doesn't even compare.

I also feel like my trauma has been resurfacing lately, or maybe I'm just becoming aware of it. Dylan and I started watching *Pen15*, a show about being in middle school in 2000. I like the show, but it's hard to watch. I don't like thinking about my childhood. It makes me feel deeply uncomfortable and sad. Recently I've been thinking about my anxiety and how it is shaped by my past experiences and trauma. Like the way I'm always expecting to get hurt and die. How jumpy I am walking around my neighborhood. How I imagine strangers trying to punch or stab me. I'm always on edge, waiting for the worst possible thing to happen.

I've thought for a while that I'm fine or that I'm "healed" because I no longer self-harm or have an eating disorder, suicidal ideation, or any of the other intensities that I experienced in the wake of my sister's death. I don't think about Alaina much at all anymore, which in and of itself, is probably part of the problem. I've been compartmentalizing, and when these feeling-memories surface it can be difficult and painful. I'm learning that anxiety doesn't always look like racing thoughts, palpitations, and insomnia. Sometimes anxiety looks like feeling blank—not feeling anything at all—not having the desire to do much or see people. It makes it hard to connect with others, especially loved ones. It makes me shy away from affection, especially kissing. I can't be present. It's hard to be grounded in my body and share that with others. It leaves me wanting to sleep, feeling overwhelmed, and wanting to check out. To smoke weed and watch shows and disengage.

April 1, 2019

A few updates from camping.

Being off the grid for a few days felt good and grounding for my mental health. I was able to process how I've been feeling triggered over the past few months, and the impacts on my energy and feelings. I think my dream about Alaina and then a conversation with my mom really made Alaina's suicide resurface for me. Even before that, I've been feeling sensitive since watching a graphic suicide scene in a Netflix movie with Dylan. The scene kept replaying in my head at random times, and I remember during a nice romantic moment with Tiana on a rooftop in LA, imagining a body falling off the side of the roof and splattering against the pavement. When we started watching *Russian Doll* a month later with all its violent deaths, I felt myself feeling triggered again. Needing some time before moving on to the next episode.

I'm glad I've realized what's been going on with me because I was blaming myself a lot and feeling bad for not having more energy, for not wanting to be sweet and affectionate with my partners. It's also enlightening to better understand what my trauma/anxiety looks like and how it works. Being triggered is not just having a PTSD-like flashback of past experiences; it can be a weight in the pit of your stomach that drags you down and makes it harder to do anything. This weight is sometimes amorphous, difficult to pinpoint, yet it's solid, sturdy, and persistent.

It felt good to be off social media for a few days. When we regained Wi-Fi and cell service, I was not ready to look at my phone. For the first day back, even messages on Facebook were something that signaled work—I didn't want to look. I was able to be more aware of how shitty and tired I usually feel after scrolling through my feed. I want to be more intentional about moving off these platforms, especially after my conversation with Tiana about what's been going on in their friend group—people who posture as pro-transformative justice are trashing a friend who made a mistake but doesn't deserve to be dragged publicly online. It's another reminder that what someone posts is not a guarantee of how they live out their values.

I checked in with my priorities and what's important in life. I place so much pressure on myself to do all the things, be friendly with everyone, raise money, make things happen, do fieldwork, and write a great dissertation. But at the end of the day, what really matters to me are my relationships. That I'm nurturing connections with the people who I love, checking in on them, and offering support. It also matters to me to show up for others in the community. But that doesn't need to be connected to my ego, whether others like me, or whether I get recognized for the work.

May 5, 2019

Woke up feeling incredibly sad and drained today. I tried to spend time with Tiana, but I just needed to be home. I knew my dogs would be comforting.

May 8, 2019

Woke up drained and tired again today, which has been the case recently. I was congested this morning and my throat was sore, so I think I'm getting sick. Somehow, knowing that I'm physically unwell makes me feel better for being so tired recently. I know I shouldn't need an excuse to rest, but it's helpful, nonetheless. It's interesting, though, because my lack of energy could be equally due to the stress and sadness I felt around recent community drama. I know when I was feeling pretty triggered and down the past few months, that translated into a lack of energy and motivation.

May 22, 2019

This has been a rough week, with a lot of community fallout and infighting. I'm feeling like my experiences "being in community" have been riddled with heartbreak and disappointment. I've been trying my best to create space for people, to provide emotional support, to fundraise, and to help folks meet their basic needs. But there is not adequate support—for the people who need care, and for the people providing care. It feels like it's the same tiny network of people who are willing to show up for things. And many of those people aren't willing to take on the stress and responsibility of leadership roles, just to fill in as support every once in a while.

I feel like no matter how thoughtful, respectful, or careful I try to be, there's always someone who is dissatisfied, hurt, upset, or angry. I know this isn't my fault. I know a lot of this is not about me. But I can't help but be worn down over time. To think of how much easier my life would be if I just withdrew from community. If I became like other people, who just worry about their jobs, family, and close friends—not all the queers and trans folks living in their city, state, or world. A life without a million entanglements and responsibilities just sounds so .... peaceful.

June 13, 2019

Today is turning into a surprisingly good day. Yesterday, I was plagued with anxiety, feeling down, my mind racing, trying to understand all the fallout that happened recently with a close friend. I got an endorphin rush after I exercised in the evening. For the first time in a while, I was able to just shut off my thoughts and be in my body, moving my body, remembering what it is to feel good. Tiana and I went out to dinner, sat next to each other in booths, talked about our day, and processed what's been going on with me and our thoughts about identity politics in San Diego. Afterward, we laid with the dogs, then went back to their house to melt into the warmth and comfort of queer intimacy. I touched them and told them what I love about them—and I apologized for the times I'm feeling too jaded and cynical to share in their awe and wonder for simple things. I need to use those moments as a reminder to bring myself back, to recognize everyday pleasures, and give thanks for little moments of coincidence, and beauty.

I picked up an Iranian asylum seeker from Amtrak today. I wondered about the potential discomfort embedded in meeting a stranger and riding along the highway together. But I immediately sensed his warmth and felt comfort in our mutual humanity. We talked about the family housing him here in California and where he's going next. He's been in the United States since January but was held in detention until last week. His friend, who he traveled with, is still there. His hearing kept being delayed, one time because the judge was sick. I sense from talking to him that much of this process is about luck. He told me he does not like having to go back to this place. I can't imagine the horrors he experienced inside. I don't ask. Instead, I ask if he's had Mexican food yet. He spent many days in Mexico, waiting to cross into the United States. He wasn't a fan of the food, aside from one meat dish. He stayed near the Centro in Tijuana for nine days. It was not safe, and he did not like to go out at night. The police would constantly question them, asking to see their papers and demanding money.

We talked less as we approached the detention center, and the cars and highways grew sparser. I could sense his nervousness, the quiet, serene dread of what is yet to come. "That was my pod," he pointed as we passed a unit with a large letter J. I told him to call me when he was finished. He told me he couldn't bring a phone inside. "Is it okay if I leave my things with you?" "Of course." At first, I offered to wait in the parking lot, and circled around looking for shade, but there was none to be found. (The detention center is not a place where green things grow). He encouraged me to leave and come back later—around 2:00 p.m., or better yet, 2:30 p.m. I wished him luck and he told me that he needed it. (He didn't have a lawyer to help with his asylum paperwork). I wished I could come inside with him, so he didn't feel so alone, but it's restricted to witnesses and family. Everyone must be pre-authorized.

I drove to the beach, laid out a blanket I keep in the back of my car, and wrote:

I needed this time at the beach to recenter and get my priorities right. It is time to invest in those relationships that make me feel seen, supported, and understood. It's time to work alongside others who make me feel good about myself, good about the work. So much of our communities try to motivate care and concern through coercion—shaming—callouts. Like Tiana said, that doesn't recognize our mutual humanity. And it's counter-productive to inspiring social change. It's time to only take on projects that speak to my strengths and interests. To be better about delegation, inclusion. Treating others like they are worthy of trust, to carry some of the burdens that I alone cannot carry.

August 20, 2019

I put up a post on Instagram asking, "What gives you hope when capitalism has you feeling hopeless?" So far fifty-one people have seen it. No one has replied. I texted my friend to tell them I was really looking forward to seeing them tomorrow, that I could use their positive energy and sage advice. They texted back, "I'm not feeling very positive either. My friend just got denied reentry to the US." Fuck. I told them I was sorry, and we should just get some wine and cuddle tomorrow. "I agree. Sometimes we just have to grieve how fucked up the world is."

September 20, 2019

I'm feeling more rested, stable, and optimistic today. Dylan, Tiana, and I went camping in Ojai and just relaxed, sitting in the sun, drinking beers, smoking weed, playing games, and cuddling the dogs. I had no cell service, and it was a nice disconnect from ordinary life. Same as last time, I've been using my phone a little bit but have been feeling less seduced into the endless scrolling and don't find myself reaching for it as easily.

Being able to slow down over the summer has been a blessing. There have still been times when I've felt overwhelmed, hopeless, and tired—mostly (as my therapist pointed out) when I've pushed against systems that are unfair and leave me feeling powerless. Like when a friend was denied accommodations from a local transportation agency again, or when another friend was a victim of police brutality.

I feel like I have some fresh perspective on why self-care is so important. While folks going to therapy and taking their meds is not going to dismantle capitalism, it does get us a step closer to being in a space of healing, from which we can forge connections with others and dream of other possibilities for ourselves and our worlds. I am grateful for the opportunity I've had to do this research, to learn about myself and my compulsion to care—where that stems from, how it can be used in service of community, and how it can surface in ways that are harmful to myself and others. Care is not neutral. And healing is everyday work.

January 31, 2020

Reading through this past year of notes in the process of coding, I'm struck by how much care work I've done in the past year. My days were often split between caring acts for multiple people—picking up and dropping off medications, donations, and flyers; listening and holding space for people's experiences; advocating at appointments; sending money; dropping off food, organizing on social media; counting donated money; helping folks get testosterone; giving rides; checking in and sending love; and my daily household reproductive labor—it's a lot. And throughout this process, I always felt like I wasn't doing enough. I felt like the work was just a drop in a bucket, that the real work was bigger, more formally organized, and with more support. It's unsurprising that I was constantly teetering on the edge of burnout, that I was so resentful of community, and that I had anxiety about showing up in public.

Throughout this process, there were people who helped, but it seemed like I always had to seek it out. Rarely did someone reach out to me and ask, "What are you working on? What do you need help with right now?" On the other hand, I assumed that if people aren't showing up for the people I know and aren't responding to the posts that I post, they aren't doing their own care work. I don't know the work people do in their everyday lives. I know that a lot of white trans people do a lot of work supporting one another (but where are they for the POC? Why is it always us taking care of each other?)

I've been feeling busy lately, but it's a different kind of busy. The projects I have— Love Affair, the mutual aid workshop, my TV podcast—feel fulfilling. They feel more collective than the work I was doing previously. It doesn't feel as intimate, as emotionally draining. When I sit down with Tiana's tarot deck, I keep drawing the Four of Cups:

> The 4 of Cups is strong, but exhausted, and unwilling to part with the quiet. She is happy now—along the seaside, surrounded by her most comforting possessions. The 4 of Cups asks you to question your exhaustion. Is it due to unhappiness, disinterest, or boredom? Living in a society so complacent with injustice, the 4 of Cups asks you to transform exhaustion into your own disengaged moment of accidental self-care.

Figure 2 The "Four of Cups" tarot card from the Next World Tarot Deck, written and illustrated by Cristy C. Road. The tarot card depicts a femme in a pink robe and fuzzy slippers, looking a bit disheveled and content. The femme is sitting alone by the seaside, perhaps on a dock, surrounded by bottles of nail polish (some spilled) and notes, letters, and envelopes.

Bibliography

Arani, Alexia. *Abolitionist Care: Crip of Color Worldmaking in the U.S.-Mexico Borderlands*. UC San Diego, Doctoral dissertation. Proquest, 2022.

Freudenberger, Herbert J. "Staff Burn-Out." *Journal of Social Issues* 30 (1974): 159–65.

Hersey, Tricia. *Rest Is Resistance: A Manifesto*. New York: Little, Brown Spark, 2022.

Kim, Jina B., and Sami Schalk. "Reclaiming the Radical Politics of Self-Care: A Crip-of-Color Critique." *The South Atlantic Quarterly* 120, no. 2 (2021): 325–42.

Maslach, Christina. "Burned-Out." *Human Behavior* 5 (1976): 16–22.

Petersen, Anne Helen. "How Millennials Became the Burnout Generation." *Buzzfeed*. January 5, 2019. https://www.buzzfeednews.com/article/annehelenpetersen/millennials-burnout-generation-debt-work.

Part II

DECOLONIZING COLLECTIVES

Figure 3 The Intertwining I by Bhasha Chakrabarti (2022).

Chapter 3

EXISTING BEYOND TIME AND PLACE: UNDERSTANDING QUEER MUSLIM VISIBILITIES ONLINE

Mardiya Siba Yahaya

On January 3, 2023, news of the murder of a well-known queer Kenyan activist, Edwin Kiprotich Chiloba, went viral on multiple social media platforms (Ombuor 2023). Chiloba's death triggered collective grief among allies and feminist activists. The messages and reactions from queer communities online were of pain and trauma from multiple and often closely related experiences of violence. Just months earlier, Sheila Lumumba, a nonbinary Kenyan person, was murdered in their home (Wepukhulu and Madegwa 2022). Queer activists in Ghana had been arrested (Akinwotu 2021) while others were kidnapped while investigating a case reported through a safety helpline they managed (Milton 2022). Meanwhile, in Zambia, the founders of a feminist group, Sistah Sistah Foundation, were arrested for "promoting homosexuality" after leading an awareness march for gender-based violence.

During the period of collective grief, trauma, and anger at the murder of yet another queer person, Kenyan politicians spearheaded gendered disinformation and homophobic violence online. As triggered by Chiloba's death, and allied communities' pain and outrage grew online, the Ugandan Parliament began deliberating on an anti-queer bill in March, which was passed in almost one week. The bill paved the way for increased homophobic violence, while simultaneously propelling transnational solidarity. The logic for regulating, monitoring, and controlling queer desires, identities, and bodies, according to many of the legislators, was that, first, queerness was against African Values, and second, that queer people should not be public actors, but should express themselves in the privacy of their homes.

Anti-queer groups and legislators claimed their discomfort with the public display of queerness because of social media. These events illuminate the *gendered construction of privacy*, a theme which is challenged through the nuanced lives of queer Muslims documented in this essay (Kovacs 2023). Whether campaigns for homophobic bills online were passed or not, they communicated which bodies should be monitored and violated (Gqola 2021). The public nature and repetition of the violent homophobic incidents and campaigns also enabled female fear (Gqola 2021) to take shape online where lines of power and safety were drawn based on one's gendered and sexual identity, instating a hierarchy of deservingness of who can experience equal humanity in shared spaces.

Putting together this manuscript while conducting research on data bodies was an incredibly difficult experience for my mind and soul. After consulting multiple academic journals, books, organizational reports, and interviews, it became increasingly clear that approaching this project must involve training my feminist senses to observe multiple stories, political events, and queer people's lives online. I assessed the logic used to enact homophobic violence in both offline and online spaces to better understand why queer people's visibility in the digital space was so threatening. In so doing, this project also provided space to filter through binary notions of pleasure and harm. Queer people online expressed rage, pain, activism, solidarity, joy, and satire. These modes of expression occur within the very space that asks them to exist "privately," allowing users to practice bodily refusals against patriarchal and masculine rules of public spaces.

As Professor Pumla Dineo Gqola (2021: 36) states, in challenging the "female fear factory," feminism becomes a dangerous job. While Gqola uses this term in the context of women who transgress patriarchal boundaries, I position resistance against the fear factory as a decolonial practice where queer Muslims craft their bodies digitally in ways that resist enforced silences, violence, and erasure in non-virtual worlds. Digital bodily practices of refusals and reclamations occur through intentionally crafted personas online, despite the commercialization of the technology platforms they rely on.

In her essay "Hearing the Silence," Panashe Chigumadzi encourages people to pay attention to the silences of historically harmed and targeted communities (Chigumadzi 2021: 226–37). Because of constant structural and interpersonal actions to invisibilize queer Muslim persons and prove their non-existence, many people conclude that they do not exist in Muslim communities. Yet Chigumadzi argues against the construction and consolidation of the self in a Euro-patriarchally recognizable manner. In this way, while online spaces allow for queerness to exist in ways that "help re-imagine the boundaries of what can be made visible, within the context of a complex politics and [practice] of visibility" (Baderoon 2015: 898), the digital world (the platform or other surveilling institutional entities) also transforms queer lives and identities into data and commodities, creating "datafied bodies," in order to be visible. I theorize the datafication of people's bodies, as readable and recognizable by technology systems as a form of violence. However, to demonstrate how queer people engage in decolonial practices through their digital bodies, I use the feminist concept of data-as-bodies[1] to depict how queer

---

1. A feminist bodies-as-data approach is used to pinpoint the specific, embodied harms of surveillance.

people online have repurposed the space and relational uses[2] of their datafied bodies to craft themselves.

Throughout the essay, I ask: what do visible online stories tell us about Muslim queer people's fragmented lives and existence? How do queer Muslim people reclaim the digital space using their digital bodies as political acts that decolonize hetero- and homo-normative visibilities on the internet? I draw extensively on interviews I conducted with queer persons who speak about the painful relationship between the digital space and their digital bodies. They shared the complicated realities of existing as a queer person online, the violence(s) enacted by other online actors and the platform as a result of their datafied self. Their stories show overlaps between the decolonial and colonial, where the digital space can enable openness and expression but at the same time reinforce and amplify heteronormativity, violence, and exploitation.

Hence, I envision decolonial bodily practices as ways queer people thrive, survive, and challenge norms that enforce hegemonic ideas that queer lives should only exist privately and are only acceptable when they belong to non-ethnic, non-Black/of color, or non-global south locations. These creators experience multiple marginalities of homophobia which they address in most of their content. To highlight their actions in response to these marginalizations, I supplement my interviews with narratives of queer expressions from three online personas—arish, tanjiro, and killua[3]—whose digital profiles and content show up in ways that demonstrate some of the approaches queer people use to reclaim the digital space to benefit them. Through their satirical video commentary, fashion, style, and informational content, arish, tanjiro, and killua push back against homonationalism,[4] a theoretical approach that reveals the tensions between racism, homophobia, Islamophobia, and xenophobia.

Decolonial practices among Muslim queer personas insists on joy, solidarity, and openly grieving in a space that seeks to erase them. They reclaim their desires, lives, and bodies by insisting on their multiplicities, while exposing liberal queer practices that force them toward an ideal queer subject who denounces their religious identity as being inherently rigid, violent, and homophobic. Reclamation happens through queer Muslims' stories and art, where their creations serve as decolonial practices that gradually "insert new insights which eventually reshuffle and do away with harmful thoughts" (Salami 2020: 71) and practices. Salami (2020: 71) invites us to envision these gradual replacements as "the garden of the mind

2. A relational approach to data governance by Salome Viljoen points out that data production in a digital economy exists to put people into population-based relations with one another. The approach argues that these relational aspects create more social value and harm within information capitalist systems.

3. These are pseudonyms for actual Tiktok creators whose creations are used in these stories.

4. The favorable association between a nationalist ideology and LGBT people. It is the creation of sexual exceptionalism along the parameters of race, nationality, and ethnicity.

where new, rare, forgotten and hybrid trees, herbs and flowers are planted that do away with the poison ivy in due course." As Salami (2020) says, while there is a time and place for the removal of violence and coloniality, queer Muslims' personas, stories, art, and subcultures actively and subtly reshape our spaces by repurposing capitalist-mediated spaces like social media to their benefit. By expressing and performing identity through fashion and redefining the concept of "home," they reclaim their lives and experiences by constructing their digital self in manners that are unrecognizable to heteropatriarchal sensibilities.

Digital Bodies as Collective Belonging in a Datafied Society

Queer, online counterpublics provide possibilities for queer people to craft their identities in specific, anonymized ways, which many prefer. The digital also enables queer folks to express themselves through alternative fashion, form friendships, and find relationships. Through digital media and technologies, queer people can express the essence of queerness, that is, exist in multiplicities and resist the injunction that, to "belong as citizens, they are required to fit in 'natural' sexual roles" (Baderoon 2015: 901). As such, the digital becomes a rare opportunity to craft identities and exist fluidly beyond physical boundaries. Queer people, "in order to attain a sense of belonging ... carve out new spaces of being"(Mclean 2014: 8).

However, queer Muslim creators have also realized that the experiences of the digital body have far more violent realities than many had anticipated. Earlier conceptualizations of queer online counterpublics were of "safe spaces to organize, exist and invent counter-experiences and discourse" (Fraser 2007: 7–30). McLean (2014) referred to this as a "cyber shelter," the organizing and crafting of digital bodies and identities by queer people to escape the violence and persecution they experience in their physical environment. This was quickly marred by design injustices, constant surveillance, and technologies reproducing gendered harm, violence, and exclusion. People seeking to harm queer folks found their way into these spaces to abuse queer users.

Meanwhile, an information capitalist society, where platforms profit from popularity and virality, incentivizes disrupting these intentionally crafted safe spaces. For example, when a person shares a TikTok video, their account is made public to the viewer. The user may intend for the viewer to watch what was shared, but not have access to their account name, making it difficult for users to protect their online profiles. Artificial intelligence (AI)-powered websites may also provide interest groups with a person's digital footprint beyond being searchable via Google. This presents one way in which Jasbir Puar (2016) asserts that our datafied body appears well before our actual bodies and is used to make decisions on our lives. Thus, our bodies become searchable, accessible, and usable from a distance in a timeless manner. Such forms of datafication turn people into commodities for behavioral surveillance, which also involves training machines to build more technologies and products dubbed as AI and selling data to institutions or companies. Selling or using data to create profitable marketing and products becomes the value generated from datafication which relies on behavioral surveillance to observe, extract, and collate and assess data into a commodity. Datafication is a commodified resource to depict how bodies are reduced to data-points (Radhakrishnan 2020) in a manner that is machine readable (Srinivasan and Johri 2013). To be made public in this manner, our lives, bodies, and identities need to exist and be managed through information flows between "data subjects and data collectors" (Viljoen 2020).

Queer people also often experience digital technologies as artifacts that misgender or harm them. In other words, a datafied space where private companies design, govern, and mediate our communication and social expression for profit complicates the concept of a "cyber shelter" or digital counterpublic. People who use digital spaces, including social media, are made accessible to individuals and institutions alike. In this context, for queer Muslim people, creating multiple separations of the self even within digital spaces can be an important way to protect themselves and limit how much information an individual observer may gather from their online profiles.

Despite the digital body and creation of data bodies emerging from exploitative, violent, and discriminatory practices that lie at the contours of a capitalist information economy and a political economy of hate, there are many queer people who insist on presenting their full selves online. The digital offers some sense of intentionality in how people design their presence, especially when they are aware that their data is being collected for multiple reasons unknown to them. Thus, the intentionality in how people might craft themselves becomes a way of reinstating autonomy. They insist on expressing solidarity, rendering violence against them and erasure as "strange" through online outrage, discourses that challenge homonationalism, and showcasing intimate love and joy.

Queer Muslims' Crafting through Dance, Alternative Fashion, and Satire

As a gender non-conforming person I am only allowed to exist in the past or the future. As a future gender, and a pre-colonial relic, but girl, I am here right now
@/alokvmenon

TikTok is designed for a person's video to pop up on your *For You* page based on your positionality within their algorithms. This was also how I came to find the creators killua, arish, and tanjiro. It was an exciting experience, at first, to come across arish's videos. Yet, when I found Killua's video, it was of them sharing that being queer and Muslim meant living alone with hateful comments targeted at them. They later turned off the comments for their post and other videos which had more than a certain number of shares, saves, and likes.

In November 2022, I watched a satirical TikTok video by a famous South African creator who mocked people asking them when they are going *home* for the holidays with the caption, "Some of us are gay, and there is no home." In many African countries, such as South Africa, during the month of December, many people leave the cities in which they work to spend the festive season or holiday with their family. While these practices are not unique to South Africa, in my adult life, I experienced the idea of "going home" during December as holding cultural significance, embedded in multiple histories. In a similar story, a Somali queer TikToker, referred to as killua, also shared a video claiming that because they are openly queer, they have to live alone. Both stories show how queer Muslim people lose their known and immediate communities, forcing them into isolation and to create new lives, versions of themselves, and grow communities elsewhere. killua, unlike the two other creators I discuss below, mostly post on their "alternative" style of fashion tattoos and piercings using TikTok sounds in ways that resonate with their style and audience. For killua, reclaiming their body through digital experience shows up by transgressing the boundaries of how a feminine Muslim person should "look," that is without tattoos or piercings. While killua rarely directly addresses queerness on their video, all three creators have queer Muslim in their bios, which instantly creates an expectation for anyone visiting their profile. Through dance, sarcastic responses, and expressions, queer Muslim creators share deeply painful aspects of their lives, which are often the experiences of many queer folks. Their videos reveal how younger creators are trying to redefine the concept of *home* to become spaces they intentionally create with their chosen community.

Another creator, arish, shares that they are not only queer, but also neurodivergent. arish combines alternative fashion, dramatic makeup choices, sounds, and captions to communicate irony. Their specific video refers to the intersecting struggles of being Muslim, queer, nonbinary, and autistic. Many of their videos use similar TikTok sounds to provide insight into various neurodivergent experiences, how families respond to neurodivergent children and adults who do not fit within stereotypical views of certain illnesses, while using themselves as a subject. arish also shares their realities of being a nonbinary Muslim person who wears a hijab—all in no particular order. They often allude to cases where they are being invisibilized within the queer community and Muslim community, who both claim they cannot hold their spirituality while being queer. arish captions one video saying, "Yes but I think being queer and Muslim is not … " and ends with an altered Digga D song called STFU. Such videos point to the multiple marginalities queer Muslims experience because of their gender, sexuality, race, religion, and ethnicity. They are made "foreign" by people who are considered community (Gqola 2021: 167) based on conceptions that queerness is only acceptable when it shows up within specific races and nationalities who are not Black people, Africans, or people of color. This narrative shows up when African legislators and politicians continuously point out that queerness is un-African.

Through a similar, yet more explicit video on the violent erasure of nonbinary people, another creator, whom I will refer to as tanjiro, explained that the world forces them into being a *non-entity*. *Non-entity* for tanjiro is when transphobic lesbians deny their belonging within the community, Muslims deny them within

Islam for their sexual orientation, Islamophobic queer people try to forcefully make them atheist, and people from their own ethnic community attempt to change their ethnicity because of their gendered and sexual identity. tanjiro being Palestinian also experiences people who deny their existence in the form of political recognition in the world. They end their video by satirically claiming they are pretty *hot* for a person who does not exist. Their comment on being *hot,* in my analysis, represents an exaggerated visibility, where a person garners more public attention than they intend for their desirable features.

All three creators explore tensions between homophobia within the Muslim community, as well as racism, xenophobia, apartheid, and Islamophobia inspired by homonationalist rhetoric. They point to the ways queer persons must align themselves with the ideals of certain global powers to be legitimately nonconforming. On one end, they experience violence and exclusion from other Muslims who invisibilize queer people because they believe that queers cannot exist in Islam. But they also navigate a queer community that believes that a person cannot be queer *and* be spiritually Muslim *and* of a certain ethnicity—thus, arishi's STFU video, and killua's comment on being a *non-entity.* In these instances, we see how the racism of homophobia is "a crucial dimension to coloniality, where racial differentiation denies humanity" (Lugones 2010: 748). The conversation on cultural values as synonymous with homophobia demonstrates how successful the projection of coloniality of gender has been and remains.

In response, all the creators use satire through trends such as "side eye"[5] and music to mock people who either ask them how they can be queer and Muslim, or queer and religious. The creators expose a specific type of homophobia in the Muslim community that means you only secure your belonging in a community when you fit within "natural" roles, which are often synonymous with heterosexuality. Meanwhile, through these stories and TikTok videos, killua, arish, and tanjiro demonstrate how their multiple, intersecting identities are considered contradictory within the queer community and how their existence is subjected to Euro-patriarchal structures of being.

These creators illuminate Puar's argument that "foregrounds the proliferation, occupation, and suppression of queerness in relation to patriotism, war, torture, security, death, terror, terrorism, detention, and deportation, themes usually imagined as devoid of connection to sexual politics in general and queer politics in particular" (Puar 2018: 21). Alternatively, queer Muslim creators openly express these contradictions, while sharing that by embracing their spirituality and ethnicity, they are considered betrayers of the nations that gave them rights to be *liberated.* On the other hand, their Muslim communities consider them aligned with imperialist nations.

Popular creators also use trendy music and commentary sounds to explain that they have existed within the space and critique people who claim not to *see* them.

5. "Side eye" is a term, lingo, or reaction people on Tik Tok use to communicate disapproval for a comment, question, or action by another person.

On TikTok, various queer Muslims share videos of themselves with their partners. The videos give us glimpses of mundane activities such as picnics, date nights, owning plants, a partner sulking or being goofy. A recent trend where people posted that they would want to see more "masc hijabis" was also a source of play and pleasure. With more queer Muslims showing up on Tiktok, however, come more queerphobic comments. Some *masc* hijabis who had never openly shared their sexuality online have to endure comments that make assumptions or slurs at them for supposedly "imitating" a man, which should be haram. These expose issues of gendered social control, where anyone who is nonconforming, whether queer or not, is considered a threat within a heteronational society. Whatever the range of emotional responses to this content, stories and videos shared by queer Muslim creators move the privatization of queerness into the public—where not only affirmation, but also violence and homophobia can occur.

killua, arish, and Tanjiro all highlight the complexities of community, violence, and pleasure. Here they reiterate, consciously and subconsciously, that they exist now, in the tensions of various socio-political realities. The stories of these creators demonstrate stories of survival and thriving (Jack and Avle 2021) beyond the gendered political harms reproduced within the designs and arrangements of technologies. Thriving and surviving also manifest through various digital personas collaborating on a video, while protecting others within their community. These forms of solidarity, survival, and protections are similar to traditional practices of resistance and refusals, such as when Awlad' Ali Bedouin women use their gender-segregated spaces to enact minor defiances of enforced restrictions, making mockery of men and manhood through music and poetry, while protecting each other from harm (Abu-lughod 1990: 41–55).

Online, too, surviving consists of daily practices and responses that expose and challenge gendered violence. Their survival stories are also told through satire and play, where they show that they lost significant community members in the form of a biological family and had to reimagine and reassess these spaces for themselves. These stories represent the painful aspects of existing and performing an identity considered contradictory. However, queer Muslim creators thrive by demonstrating that the digital body, which is often expected to appear perfectly curated in normative ways, can center complex stories. Enabled by the digital cultures of TikTok, curating and crafting, as tanjiro, arish, and killua show us, can be intentionally messy.

Queer Digital Bodies and Self-Fragmentation

When queer persons experience multiple forms of oppression because their identity challenges patriarchal designs and enforcements of gender and sexuality, they are compelled to hide aspects of their lives while creating alternative ways to be visible. In other words, the violated and oppressed body lives, performs its identity, and exists in fragments. Yet, at least when it comes to their digital personas, queer creators show how fragmentation is a way to survive physically and digitally. Some queer people also use fragmentation as a reflective and healing opportunity.

Through conversations I had with two queer creative technologists whom I met in Kenya, the first, Okong'o, explained that his virtual self is categorized into two. One, he described as his pseudo virtual self, where he exists as a carefully curated personality to filter out parts of himself. Second, what he considered the more real aspect of himself is only accessible to another person when trust and the feeling of safety develop. Nerima, his colleague, on the other hand, considered their digital body as a performance of the self where aspects of their lives which they could not express in the offline space manifested in their online expression. For Nerima, performance connects with practices of drama and performance studies in which they specialized, and they explore within digital spaces an attempt to reconcile the violence and struggles of a queerphobic society with practices of healing. To Nerima, their digital body is where they experiment and illustrate their artistic persona and how growing up with the internet has shaped their identity.

Both Okong'o and Nerima point out that the digital body and its realities are as complicated as what exists offline and *physically*. For instance, Okong'o shared that supposed counterpublics have been used by states, queerphobic, and other queer people to surveil and harm more vulnerable groups within the community. Grindr and other queer specific dating apps have been used as sites of violence against queer people, at the social and platform level—yet the platform companies benefit from queer expressions, engagement, and culture. Nerima shared that their interactions on Instagram significantly shaped how they came to perceive their embodied selves. While their "embodied self" continues to be a concept they grapple with and reshape, their accounts highlight that technologies have come to influence how queer Muslim creators perform and relate to their identities. Creating spaces of belonging, even fragmented ones, can produce pleasure, yet Nerima and Okong'o also demonstrate that while queer people create the digital body and can find temporal routes for healing and pleasure, at the structural design and platform level, harm is being reproduced and the queer person's digital body is being exploited. Like most of the queer Tiktokers I examined, Nerima's dramatic fashion and makeup are considered "alternative." Through their attempt to reconcile the digital with the physical body, they experienced violence from people who would shame, harass, and assault them, forcing Nerima to keep parts of themselves fragmented—their digital body experience apart from the physical.

Datafication, as a particular form of violence induced by surveillance and abstracted algorithmic decision making and operations, helps frame Nerima and Okong'o's insight that the queer digital body is exploited. Okong'o observed that platforms that benefit from queer engagement relate to the broader commodification and appropriation of Black and queer practices in popular culture today. Co-opted versions of *street* fashion and *drag* abound online. However, when people like Nerima perform their identity in this manner, they experience violence. Nerima also explained that there is a link between the digital body that is constantly being stolen from and the relation between violence toward their avatar and their physical body. Unknown users can take their content and share it with family and close community, for example. This way, the digital body does not remain within the realm of the digital, but comes to affect their life and relationships with people offline as well, making fragmentation a difficult practice to maintain. Theft of digital bodies also happens when the art and work of queer Muslim creators are used by technology platforms in multiple ways unknown to the user. Nerima indicated that the Black queer digital body is only allowed a little leeway to push against boundaries within heteropatriarchal societies. A Black queer person's creative expression moves from the online persona whose culture is powering digital platforms, to a controlled and moderated body whose post is taken down and constantly flagged, but their data continues to be utilized regardless.

Okong'o and Nerima's stories embody the constant negotiations queer people must make online, in gendered digital and analog societies and in relation to techno-empires that own and moderate digital spaces. These conflicts and negotiations happen when they are actively and carefully weaving their complex lives into our present and archival futures. Still, despite the datafication of the body and the violence it reconfigures, queer Muslims use the online space as a means to craft a fragmented aspect of their lives, moving the issues and violence they experience from the political margins to "public" spaces, while revealing ongoing homonationalist tensions, violence, and discrimination that they face.

Conclusion: Who Gets to Claim Decoloniality?

A shared construction or definition of a decolonial digital body, technology or conditions for decolonial data practices, remains a difficult task. The violent and exploitative nature of data production, use and practice, the commercialization of queer visibilities, and the imperialist and Islamophobic practices and rhetoric associated with these *visibilities* raise questions for feminist and queer communities about who can claim decoloniality within the digital. However, for the people I spoke with, decoloniality consisted of collective practices derived from words such as the *autonomy* to express oneself and one's desires *without violence, exploitation,* and with *community protection.*

Given that this work draws from performances of gendered and sexual identity through various artistic modes facilitated by technology, I have highlighted practices of decolonial digital bodies from artists' crafting of healing, pleasure, and satire amid events that communicate otherwise. In my conversation with Nerima, they shared the work of Tabita Rezaire[6] as inspirational to how they practice digitality. They cited that, just like Rezaire, they are an "agent of healing [who] uses art as a means to unfold the soul" (Rezaire,nd). I similarly explore and frame

6. Tabita Rezaire is an artist based in Cayenne, French Guyana. Her work is rooted in time-spaces where technology and spirituality intersect as fertile ground to nourish visions of connection and emancipation.

the queer digital bodies of Muslims as illuminating de/coloniality by highlighting the maneuvers between joy, pleasure, Islamophobia, homophobia, and the imperialist co-option of queerness through creative art and fashion via TikTok. These stories of thriving, surviving, and embedding identities within techno-empires that erase or commercialize them illustrate decoloniality as a continuous practice that pushes against a specific form of arrival.

Despite increasing state and interpersonal homophobia and violence that ask them not to be visible and not to exist, queer creators use these same spaces to express collective outrage, solidarity, and pain. By recreating ideas of home and expressing intimate partnerships even during Ramadan, when forbidden intimacies are often put on hold, they contribute to rendering the "female fear factory" unnatural. Queer Muslim creators and technologists embed themselves in our histories, present, and futures, in no particular order, without waiting for approval.

Bibliography

Abu-Lughod, Lila. "The Romance of Resistance: Tracing Transformations of Power through Bedouin Women." *American Ethnologist* 17, no. 1 (1990): 41–55. https://doi.org/10.1525/ae.1990.17.1.02a00030.

Akinwotu, Emmanuel. "Outcry after 21 People Arrested in Ghana for 'Advocating LGBTQ Activities.'" *The Guardian*, May 25, 2021. https://www.theguardian.com/world/2021/may/24/outcry-people-arrested-ghana-advocating-lgbtq-activities.

Baderoon, Gabeba. "'I Compose Myself': Lesbian Muslim Autobiographies and the Craft of Self-Writing in South Africa." *Journal of the American Academy of Religion* 83, no. 4 (2015): 897–915. https://doi.org/10.1093/jaarel/lfv075.

Fraser, Nancy. "Special Section: Transnational Public Sphere: Transnationalizing the Public Sphere." *Theory, Culture & Society* 24, no. 4 (2007): 7–30. https://doi.org/10.1177/0263276407080090.

Fraser, Nancy, and Kate Nash. *Transnationalizing the Public Sphere*. Amsterdam: Amsterdam University Press, 2014.

Gqola, Pumla Dineo. *Female Fear Factory*. Cape Town: Melinda Ferguson Books, 2021.

Iyer, Neema, and Garnett Achieng. "Inclusion Not Just an Add On." *Pollicy.Org*. 2022. https://pollicy.org/resource/inclusion-not-just-an-add-on/.

Jack, Margaret, and Seyram Avle. "A Feminist Geopolitics of Technology." *Global Perspectives* 2, no. 1 (2021): 3–5. https://doi.org/10.1525/gp.2021.24398.

JohnBoals. "Jasbir Puar_ Regimes of Surveillance—Cosmologics Magazine." *Scribd*, n.d. https://www.scribd.com/document/297838582/Jasbir-Puar-Regimes-of-Surveillance-Cosmologics-Magazine.

Kovacs, Anja. "Searching for a Room of One's Own in Cyberspace: Datafication and the Global Feminisation of Privacy." *Social Science Research Network*, January 1, 2023. https://doi.org/10.2139/ssrn.4387652.

Lewis, Desiree, Gabeba Baderoon, and Panashe Chigumadzi. *Surfacing: On Being Black and Feminist in South Africa*. First ed. 2021. Reprint, Johannesburg: Wits University Press, 2021.

Lugones, María. "Toward a Decolonial Feminism." *Hypatia: A Journal of Feminist Philosophy* 25, no. 4 (2010): 742–59. https://doi.org/10.1111/j.1527-2001.2010.01137.x.

McLean, Nyx. "Considering the Internet as Enabling Queer Publics/ Counter Publics." *Spheres: Journal for Digital Cultures* 1 (2014): 1–12. https://doi.org/10.25969/mediarep/3823.

Milton, Josh, and Josh Milton. "Violent Homophobic Thugs Held Ghanaian LGBTQ+ Activist Hostage: 'Annoy Us and We'll Kill You.'" *PinkNews | Latest Lesbian, Gay, Bi and Trans News | LGBTQ+ News*, August 28, 2022. https://www.thepinknews.com/2022/08/28/rightify-ghana-held-hostage/.

openDemocracy. "Hopes for Justice as Man Charged with Lesbian's Murder." n.d. https://www.opendemocracy.net/en/5050/sheila-lumumba-lesbian-murder-rape-kenyan-police/.

openDemocracy. "'We Only Have Each Other': LGBTIQ Kenya Mourns Again." n.d. https://www.opendemocracy.net/en/5050/edwin-chiloba-murder-lgbtiq-kenya-africa/.

Puar, Jasbir. *Terrorist Assemblages: Homonationalism in Queer Times* (Next Wave: New Directions in Women's Studies). Anniversary, Tenth Anniversary. Durham and London: Duke University Press Books, 2018.

Radhakrishnan, Radhika. "'I Took Allah's Name and Stepped Out': Bodies, Data and Embodied Experiences of Surveillance and Control during COVID-19 in India." *Internet Democracy Project*. Data Governance Network, 2020. https://internetdemocracy.in/reports/i-took-allahs-name-and-stepped-out-bodies-data-and-embodied-experiences-of-surveillance-and-control-during-covid-19-in-india (accessed March 1, 2023).

Salami, Minna. *Sensuous Knowledge: A Black Feminist Approach for Everyone.* New York: Amistad, an Imprint of Harpercolinspublishers, 2020.

Schlesinger, Philip. "After the Post-Public Sphere." *Media, Culture & Society* 42, no. 7–8 (2020): 1545–63. https://doi.org/10.1177/0163443720948003.

Srinivasan, Janaki, and Aditya Johri. "Creating Machine Readable Men." *Proceedings of the Sixth International Conference on Information and Communication Technologies and Development: Full Papers* 11, no. 13 (2013): 101–12. https://doi.org/10.1145/2516604.2516625.

tabitarezaire.com. "Info." n.d. https://tabitarezaire.com/info.

Viljoen, Salome. "Democratic Data: A Relational Theory for Data Governance." *Social Science Research Network*, November 11, 2020. https://doi.org/10.2139/ssrn.3727562.

Chapter 4

DECOLONIZED BODIES OF LAND AND CHILDREN: SARAH WINNEMUCCA'S LANDBACK PROJECT IN *LIFE AMONG THE PIUTES*

Kristine Amanda Koyama

Nearly a century before the Native-led activism of the mid-twentieth century, nineteenth-century Paiute[1] activist, educator, and lecturer Sarah Winnemucca petitioned the US Congress to return her people's land and acknowledge their autonomy to govern themselves. Winnemucca's congressional petition demands restitution for "that portion" of her tribe "arbitrarily removed from the Malheur Reservation," an event that caused many families to be "ruthlessly separated" so that they "never ceased to pine for husbands, wives, and children" (1883: 108). In 1872, the US government designated the Malheur Reservation for the Paiute people. During the years Malheur was operational, the US government assigned federal agents to manage the Paiute people. These agents stole the people's rations and forced them into a state of dependence. Since their arrival in the region in the 1840s, white settlers polluted food sources and waterways that were essential to the tribe's way of life and economic sustainability. After the 1878 Bannock War,[2] the United States disbanded the reservation and relocated over 500 Paiute citizens to the Yakima Reservation in response to the demands of settlers seeking the land for themselves.

Invested in redressing these injustices and maintaining Paiute sovereignty to govern Malheur, Winnemucca published her autobiography, *Life Among the Piutes*, in 1883. The narrative begins with Sarah's[3] childhood, engaging readers in intimate details about her upbringing, family relationships, education, and homelife before providing a Paiute-centered account of the Bannock War that pinpoints settler violence as the underlying cause, a reality she knew well from her career as a US

---

1. "Piute" was the common spelling of the tribe in the nineteenth century.

2. This war was fought by Bannock and Paiute people resisting the encroachment of Euro-American settlers and the US government on their traditional lands and resources.

3. I use "Sarah" to distinguish Winnemucca's authorial voice from her narrativization of herself in *Life*.

military interpreter and advocate for her people. At the end of *Life*, Winnemucca includes a copy of her congressional petition, which she encourages her middle-class, white American readers to copy, sign, and canvas.

In so doing, Winnemucca teaches her nineteenth-century audience to read and feel the land from an Indigenous critical center. Her autobiography interrogates settler assumptions about land inheritance through traditions that tell of "the beginning of the world" (1883: 9), how the Paiutes came to be "called Pine-nut eaters" (1883: 37), and why "we Piutes have always lived on the river" (1883: 38). These stories place Winnemucca's people on the land since time immemorial and attest to Paiute people's roles as stewards of the land. As readers of *Life* imaginatively grow alongside Sarah, they become invested in Winnemucca's decolonizing project. By signing and canvassing her petition, they actively engage in the real-world civic actions necessary to restore Paiute sovereignty and reunite Paiute people with their ancestral land.

In this essay, I examine how Winnemucca evokes culturally situated applications of "the sentimental" to engage readers in a decolonizing project that both transforms their embodied knowledge—changing what they know and how they feel about the land—while energizing their investments in returning governance of the land to its original inhabitants. That is, I explore how Winnemucca initiates a landback movement through a sentimental coming-of-age narrative, such as her dexterous use of emotionally charged scenes which convey Paiute national history by underscoring the intimate and essential relationship between Paiute people and the land. For instance, Winnemucca relays the Paiute perspective of the Bannock War by leveraging a tearful public reunion between herself (as an adult) and her father who, upon seeing her, cries: "Oh, my poor child! I thought I never would see you," and as Sarah looks up, she sees not only her father's "tears were running down his cheeks" but also that there were "tears in everyone's eyes" (1883: 83).

In conventional, nineteenth-century literature, teary-eyed reunions like this elicited emotional responses from white, middle-class readers as a catalyst for embodied learning. In *The Masochistic Pleasures of Sentimental Literature*, Marianne Noble explains the long-standing and wide-reaching cultural impact of the sentimental mode of aesthetic expression, behaviors, and ideology emergent from the eighteenth-century Scottish Common Sense school of philosophy, which understood that "the moral sense was an embodied, feeling-based form of cognition that seemed to many people to redeem both human nature and the human body" (2000: 63). Noble finds that "sentimental plots are built around a quest for unity, and sentimental tears are shed over sundered unions" (2000: 65), a mechanism Winnemucca evokes through Sarah's reunion with her tribe.

Engaging in the culture of sentiment for the project of decolonization was politically savvy because of how the sentimental mode served the paternalistic sympathies of white reformers. Shirley Samuels underscores in her seminal work, *The Culture of Sentiment: Race, Gender, and Sentimentality in Nineteenth-Century America* that, at the time, the cultural power of sentimentality delineates "sympathy ... across race, class, and gender lines" (1992: 6). Its power to bring readers to tears allowed reformers to evoke sympathy for marginalized groups, and when employed by white authors, these sympathies often resulted in paternalistic benevolence that served assimilationist agendas. In her study *Tender Violence*, Lauren Wexler examines how the Hampton Institute in Virginia used sentimental aesthetics in their "before and after" photos of Indigenous girls to promote their capacity to quickly assimilate children (2000: 109–11).

However, Winnemucca's use of sentimentality was radically different from that of US reformers who used it to form assimilationist arguments and justify settler colonialism. After reuniting with her people, Sarah recalls "who was killed, what their names were, and how many prisoners we had, about our baby, and the four women, and the poor blind woman, who was scalped, and about poor Egan, who was cut to pieces" (1883: 84). Recounting this history punctuates the relief readers may feel at Sarah's reunion with her tribe with an awareness of the ongoing violence of separation the surviving members must endure as the United States displaces them to Yakima. Scholars like Malea Powell (Indiana Miami and Eastern Shawnee), Cari M. Carpenter, and Siobhan Senier have also shown that Winnemucca was intimately aware of the power of the sentimental to influence American hearts and minds. Senier argues that throughout her career Winnemucca issues "powerful critiques of allotment and assimilation" (2001: 75) with language that Powell argues is "deliberately rhetorical," because *Life* doesn't so much tell about Winnemucca's life as it does present a version of her life in order to persuade her audience to help the Paiutes" (2001: 406). Carpenter, likewise, finds that in Winnemucca's Congressional speeches in the Eastern states, "spectators' tears were her goal, which she often achieved" (2014: 7). Winnemucca's sophisticated use of sentimental conventions controlled her audience's emotional currents, bringing them from bouts of laughter to waves of tears with impassioned calls for justice.

Before nineteenth-century white readers could embrace this path to justice, Winnemucca needed to unsettle their existing view of the land's history. They could not simply be brought to tears, but those tears must embody an understanding of why it is so detrimental to separate Indigenous peoples from the land they have always inhabited. Winnemucca was intentional when designing the petition included at the end of the book. Also written in the sentimental mode, it characterizes the United States' policies of dispossession as engines of suffering, calling attention to husbands, wives, and children who have been "ruthlessly separated," and seeks "friends who sympathize in the cause of my people" (Winnemucca 1883: 108). That is, to support Winnemucca's congressional appeal, a signer must acknowledge the Paiute nation as an autonomous body outside of the United States' authority and feel deeply about upholding the Paiute people's sovereign right to govern themselves on their ancestral land. In this way, Winnemucca's petition makes "the way to justice … easy" for her readers (Powell 2002: 409).

Putting a sentimental Paiute child at the helm of her narrative also strategically teaches her readers to unlearn American entitlement to land management. Karen Sanchez-Eppler's excellent study of Antebellum cultural practices in *Dependent States: The Child's Part in Nineteenth-century American Culture*, shows that, throughout the nineteenth century, children, both real and literary, existed not only as "objects of socialization," but also as "forces" evocative of a "wide range of cultural and political discourses in attempts to reform, direct, or influence the nation" (2005: xv). Their influence worked alongside the cultural power of sentimentality that, according to Samuels, was largely a project "about imagining the nation's bodies and national body" (1992: 3). Popular authors of the period, including Lydia Maria Child, Catharine Sedgwick, Harriet Beecher Stowe, Susan Warner, Maria Cummings, and Louisa May Alcott, used sentimental children to map a narrative of national belonging, in part, by imagining middle-class white children as the ideal American citizens, mythologizing them as the children of the land.

Winnemucca, however, develops a uniquely Indigenous form of sentimental childhood that blends familiar coming-of-age conventions with Paiute knowledge and history. As she learns important socialization and domestic skills, Sarah hears and tells stories about the Paiute creation origins, her people's role as "the only tribe that lives in the country where Pine-nuts grow" (Winnemucca 1883: 37), and how under Paiute governance, the lakes generate many trout "weighing from two to twenty-five pounds each" (Winnemucca 1883: 38), engaging American readers in these same lessons. These stories teach them how pine nuts and trout provide physical sustenance to both human and nonhuman bodies and to see the interconnectedness and wholeness of the relationship between Paiute people and the land.

Learning the lessons that Sarah learns growing up in Paiute territory enacts what Sandra Styres (Kanien'kehá:ka) terms "literacies of the land," meaning "a critical conscious awareness and an acknowledgment of whose traditional lands we are now on" (32). Winnemucca's intentional storytelling strategies invite readers to transform their knowledge of the land's history and to root themselves in Paiute traditions. Styres insists that land as a "decolonizing praxis" works through "storied relationships … etched into the essence of every rock, tree, animal, pathway, and waterway" (2019: 30). With the knowledge from these stories, readers of *Life* become invested in Winnemucca's landback project. In the sections that follow, I examine how Paiute storytelling traditions inform Winnemucca's method for teaching these critical land lessons.

Telling Stories to Children

Northern Paiute people use stories as the primary method for passing on traditional teachings to younger generations and keeping knowledge of the land alive. Reflecting on stories shared by elders helps develop children's critical faculties. Paiute scholars and storytellers Judy Trejo and Wilson Wewa both recall the lessons they learned from the stories told by family members and community elders. Wewa credits the spontaneous or situational nature of their telling—like passing on the Paiute names for plants, places, or histories of a region—as they came across them in their travels (2017: 70).

Winnemucca similarly demonstrates the power of Indigenous storytelling practices by depicting their transformative effects on Sarah as a child. The narrative distinguishes between young Sarah's cognitive responses to conversational "talking" and "saying" versus intentional storytelling. For instance, young Sarah hides, screams, and cries to avoid interacting with settlers because she distrusts and fears them. Although Winnemucca depicts her grandfather constantly "*talking … about* the good white people" (1883: 14; emphasis added), and having "*said* everything that was good" about them, his words do not change her mind (1883: 17; emphasis added). Multiple times her grandfather "said I [Sarah] must not be afraid of the white people, for they are very good," but Sarah only responds that "they looked so very bad I could not help it" (1883: 16). Sarah has not embodied the knowledge of how to befriend white people and does not feel it possible.

After several periods of uncontrollable crying, however, her grandfather tries something different, announcing that he will "tell" Sarah about "what I did with a beautiful gift I received from my white brothers" (Winnemucca 1883: 17). "Tell" distinguishes his words from mere talk, signaling a meaningful exchange in which Sarah is expected to engage and reflect. Sarah's grandfather tells her that his "white brothers" once gave him a "beautiful" plate and they laughed at him for wearing it on his head (Winnemucca 1883: 18). Sarah's grandfather characterizes his white brothers' laughter not "to make fun" of him, but simply "because I wore the tin plate for a hat" (Winnemucca 1883: 18). Unlike when he talks and says good things about white people, her grandfather does not insist his story proves that all white people are friendly. Rather, he lets the child decide what conclusions to draw. Trejo similarly recalls that after listening to coyote stories, "we might discuss some of the tales," not because they were confusing, as "the meaning of the various stories were fairly clear," but rather to reflect on applicable takeaways (1974: 18). Likewise, Sarah "kept thinking over" her grandfather's story and is determined to "make friends with" the white people (Winnemucca 1883: 18). She never expresses a belief that all white people are friendly. Her encounters with settlers have taught her better. Sarah's choice to be friends illustrates the affective power of Paiute storytelling practices to help children think through their personal experiences and embody a new critical awareness of their roles as emerging community leaders. Furthermore, it exemplifies the power of stories to discipline children without infringing on their autonomy.

Abenaki storyteller Joseph Bruchac argues that most, if not all, Indigenous storytelling practices aim to discipline children without stirring resentment, for if you "beat a child," it might injure their spirit and "teach that child that it was right for those who were big and strong to pick on those smaller and weaker," whereas "a good story, a good lesson, would go straight to the child's heart" (1991: 38). Indigenous storytelling invites critical reflection through a principle of nonviolence. Nonviolent discipline is also essential to Winnemucca's sentimental technique because it counters the era's pedagogies of violence central to government-run boarding schools for Indigenous children. Through "before and after" photos of Indigenous children taken to these schools, Wexler argues that forcing a sentimental aesthetic, like wearing "tightly fitting Victorian dresses with lace collars ... wearing leather boots in lieu of their old soft moccasins," and "having had their braids cut off," constitutes a violent attempt at cultural erasure (2000: 111). These children, as Wexler shows, resist through acts of bodily rebellion, like subtle slouching, distant gazes, and notable disinterest in their Western-style dolls and toys, even as they are poised to appear "civilized" in photographs distributed to raise donations from the same middle-class white public that Winnemucca sought to educate.

Traditional elements of storytelling combined with a sentimental style facilitate identification with the Paiute child such that readers see the actions of white characters from an Indigenous critical perspective. Engaging in stories through identification with their "favorites among the animals" taught Trejo and her siblings "proper behavior" toward each other and elders as they reflected on her connection with those animals (1974: 69). Styres explains that land literacies gained through an embodied identification with Indigenous perspectives work by first "opening opportunities for learners to understand themselves" and then "through critical self-reflection ... [to] gain a better understanding of each other and the ways power, privilege, and colonial relations continue to inform our ways of knowing and being in the world" (2019: 26).

Winnemucca's decolonizing praxis allows readers to experience the sentimentalized Paiute child's fear of well-intentioned white characters so that they can, in turn, reflect on and recognize the ways their own attitudes and actions are complicit in the real-world injustices faced by the Paiute people. Thus, Winnemucca treats her readers with the same ethos of nonviolence that Paiute people use to educate their children, effectively undermining the pedagogies of institutionalized violence used on Indigenous children and demonstrating the transformative power of Indigenous storytelling on the bodies of those who listen.

Sentimental Land Lessons

Winnemucca also subverts conventional settler expectations about idyllic and innocent sentimental childhoods to make the disruption of Paiute land by settler invasion palpable. She states in the opening sentence of *Life* that she was "a very small child when the first white people came into our country" (Winnemucca 1883: 9). Her account of settler arrival links the dispossession of the land with a stolen childhood: Sarah must now grow up in the context of settler presence. Winnemucca likewise connects this disruption with the dispersal of Paiute bodies. From the moment settlers arrived, her "people were scattered ... over nearly all the territory now known as Nevada" (Winnemucca 1883: 9). When Winnemucca writes that dispersal happens "over nearly all the territory *now known* as Nevada," she implies "Nevada" is a name untethered to the land's ancient history or to the Paiute people who know "our country" with a different language (Winnemucca 1883: 9; emphasis added). Instilling this sense of discomfort in her audience—making the familiar "Nevada" unfamiliar—is an important aspect of Winnemucca's decolonizing praxis. Even as Winnemucca directly calls this space "Nevada," the implication of a different—long-standing—center of knowledge is apparent in her passive voice. Sarah and her people think of Paiute country as distinct from "Nevada"; thus the "now known" emphasizes how the language her people use for this territory is much older and more deeply rooted than the nomenclature of white settlers.

By implying the newness of naming the territory "Nevada," Winnemucca exposes the corrupted way settlers tell stories about the land, by arriving and naming without listening to its stories. Syilx (Okanagan) activist, artist, and writer Jeannette Armstrong explains that Indigenous languages, and thus their worldviews, live in and emerge from the earth. She learned from her father that Okanagan people "survived and thrived by listening intently … and then inventing human words to tell its stories" (1998: 176). Paiute knowledge, likewise, emerges from the earth. It exists before, after, and around settler definitions. By engaging in these linguistic maneuvers that reveal the artificiality of names like "Nevada" from the perspective of a Paiute child whose knowledge of the land predates settler arrival, Winnemucca destabilizes the metonymic hold that settler stories use to mythologize their own origins.

This move is illustrative of what Warren Cariou (Métis) has termed a "terristory," wherein Indigenous storytellers listen to and read the land in order to speak *with it*, rather than *about it* as they "shift focus from the disruption of colonialism" to the "ongoing relationship, from the deep past to the foreseen future" (2020: 5). Rather than dwell on the disruption of settler invasion, Winnemucca's terristorying highlights her people's enduring presence and deep connection with the land, underlining the ongoing nature of their stories and their role as the storytellers. Winnemucca's decolonizing praxis thus makes space for unsettling knowledge through a pedagogy of nonviolence. If willing to listen, Winnemucca's readers can become land literate from a Paiute worldview that knows the land more intimately than those who conceive of this place as "Nevada."

Every Indigenous North American tribe has their own legends and creation stories that place their people on the continent since time immemorial. In Wewa's telling of the Northern Paiute creation story, the animals called *Nuwuddu*, or first people, work together to create the land (2017: 6–8). The land is integral to Paiute creation stories because the people needed the land to survive. Their stories are shaped by the way that the people learned to live with their environment. Sometime after the land is formed, Coyote pesters the woman who was an Oriole to see inside her paosa (water jug), and opening it when she is asleep, releases all the children who begin to scatter across the earth (Wewa 2017: 9). By the time Coyote refastens the lid, "there was one boy and one girl left. So he turned the bottle upside down … pulled them out … and they were the first two human people in this world. A man and a woman" (Wewa 2017: 10). This is the creation of *Nuwu*, the second people. Following Sarah's disrupted childhood at the beginning of *Life*, she continues her sentimental land lessons by including a Paiute legend predicated on their creation story.

The legend appears in the narrative shortly after the tribe learns of the presence of white people, which causes panic. Sarah recalls her grandfather gathering the tribe together to remind them that: "'In the beginning of the world there were only four, two girls and two boys. Our forefather and mother were only two, and we are their children. You all know that a great while ago there was a happy family in this world'" (Winnemucca 1883: 9). The elder storyteller recalls, however, that "'soon [the children of the happy family] disagreed, and there was trouble,'" so their father "'separated his children by a word,'" commanding the white children to "'depart from each other'" and "'go across the mighty ocean,'" after which the "'light girl and boy disappeared'" (Winnemucca 1883: 9). Sarah's grandfather concludes by reminding the Paiute listeners that "'by-and-by the dark children grew into a large nation; and we believe it is the one we belong to, and that the nation'" (Winnemucca 1883: 9).

By including this legend, Winnemucca leverages the narrative conventions of "'intimate relationships'" and "'a quest for unity'" that Noble views as constitutive to sentimental plots (2000: 65) and uses them for two distinct decolonial purposes. First, telling this legend reaffirms the Paiute people's national identity as original, intimate caretakers of the land. Second, it reassures the Paiute people that white settlers lack the authority to claim the land as their own. This legend assumes the Paiute creation story to have occurred and unifies the national body of Paiute people around their identification with these stories. Like the Paiute creation story as told by Wewa, children in Winnemucca's legend situate Paiute people's constant and continued presence in North America since creation.

As Wewa tells it under the title "A Legend of Darker- and Lighter-skinned Children—and Prophecies of White People Coming Out East," the children's aptitudes and dispositions make the darker-skinned children better positioned as stewards of the land. Complexion thus works to establish Paiute origins in North America and situate white settlers as children returning from exile. The implication being that, as the less mature body, the white children have a lot to learn. When the father tries to teach the elder darker-skinned boy how to hunt, fish, make arrowheads, spears, fish hooks, and twine for nets, the boy does well, while his lighter-skinned sister has a "hard time listening" to her mother who "tried very earnestly to teach" her the skills of splitting willows, making baskets, weaving hats, sewing moccasins, and grinding pine nuts (Wewa 2017: 113). Similarly, when the parents have two more children, the lighter-skinned boy "acted like his mind was far away" during lessons, and the darker-skinned girl learned well "all of those things" her mother sought to teach her (Wewa 2017: 114). Although Winnemucca does not develop the children's identities, their father's act of separating the children and sending the white ones away sets each pair of children up to develop different centers of knowledge and relationships with the land now known as North America.

A Body of Nuts and Fish

When Sarah is still a child, her grandfather falls sick and dies. As they mourn the loss of a great love, storyteller, and leader, "everybody would take his dead body in their arms and weep" (Winnemucca 1883: 35). His passing lays bare what is at stake when elders who possess traditional knowledge die. Winnemucca recalls that she "was only a simple child, yet I knew what a great man he was" (1883: 35). Significantly, this is the last scene in which Winnemucca depicts herself as a child. Harnessing the heightened emotions of her grandfather's passing, Winnemucca tells one of the significant "traditions of our people," recounting how long ago, "a tribe of barbarians … used to waylay" the Paiute people, "kill[ing] and eat[ing] them," but when the Paiute people defeated these barbarians, they became "the only tribe that lives in the country where Pine-nuts grow" (1883: 37). When her grandfather passes, Sarah shifts from being a child who learns from stories to being a storyteller responsible for passing on her nation's history. This role switch emphasizes storied learning as a process that prepares children to take on roles as community leaders. Her grandfather's passing marks the inception of Winnemucca's role as an adult storyteller who historicizes her people as the nation of pine nut trees.

Referring to the tribe as the "only" ones who live where pine nuts grow is an important signifier of Paiute national sovereignty. In contrast to the prevailing view of sovereignty as rooted in the idea of Manifest Destiny and expansionist policies that charted fixed territorial boundaries on maps, Winnemucca's assertion that the Paiutes are the "only" nation among the pine nuts establishes a boundary that moves and is shaped by the ecology of these trees. Wewa also sheds light on the Paiute people's traditions with tree-defined boundaries. In "When the Animals Were Still People and Starvation Hit the Land," Wewa tells that during a period of great starvation, the people were looking everywhere for food when it was discovered that a "real fierce people" called *Pahizoho'o* possessed seeds—pine nut seeds—that could feed the Paiute people (Wewa 2017: 23). Like Winnemucca's telling, the people defeated *Pahizoho'o*, from which they acquired a single pine nut seed, which Coyote gives to Wolf "so he could 'use his power' to make more food" (Wewa 2017: 24). In the legend, "Wolf Makes Pine Nut Trees," he carries the seed in his mouth and "wherever Wolf spit, a pine nut tree would grow" (Wewa 2017: 25). Anishinabe poet, scholar, and activist Lenore Keeshig-Tobias maintains that more than "sheer entertainment," Indigenous stories act as "a record of proud Nations confident in their achievement" (qtd. in Bruchac 1991: 38). Stories of pine nuts in *Life* likewise record the many ways Paiute national identity emerges from the earth, springing up from underneath, and therefore is inseparable from its natural resources.

Pine nuts are both a symbolic and geographic marker of Paiute sovereignty because their stories keep knowledge of the land alive and mark the boundaries of the Paiute nation. As the only people in the region with pine nut trees, the Paiute people possess traditions about gathering and surviving off this natural resource. Several times in *Life,* Winnemucca's tribe goes to the mountains to avoid bloodshed by white settlers. While in the mountains, the pine nut trees protect them, and the harvest of nuts sustain them through the winter. Tribal historian Edward C. Johnson (Northern Paiute) records that as a staple of the people's diet, the pine nut produces critical traditions marked by the "dancing, gambling, and games [that] took place" at the yearly harvests (1975: 10–11). Pine nut trees are members of the tribe because they provide protection and sustenance as well as participate in collective celebrations, an Indigenous concept of belonging Robin Wall Kimmerer (Citizen Potawatomi Nation) discusses at length in her book *Braiding Sweetgrass* (2013: 168). As citizens themselves, the pine nut trees contribute to the health and well-being of the other inhabitants of the region, making it possible to celebrate an abundant harvest together.

Just as pine nuts signal Paiute stewardship of the land, trout fishing represents the strength of the Paiute nation's economy. In the chapter, "Pyramid and Muddy Lakes Reservations," Winnemucca critiques US railroad policies that cut off the tribe's access to traditional waters that provide them with food, economic strength, and cultural practices essential to their survival:

> THIS reservation, given in 1860, was at first sixty miles long and fifteen wide. The line is where the railroad now crosses the river, and it takes in two beautiful lakes, one called Pyramid Lake, and the one on the eastern side, Muddy Lake … We Piutes have always lived on the river, because out of those two lakes we caught beautiful mountain trout, weighing from two to twenty-five pounds each, which would give us a good income if we had it all, as at first. Since the railroad … the white people have taken all the best part of the reservation … and one of the lakes also.
>
> (1883: 38)

According to Chief Harry in *The Paiutes of Pyramid Lake*, the Paiute people ran massive commercial fishing operations that afforded them enough food to both sustain their tribe and engage in trade with enough to replenish the waters each year (Hermann 1972: 193). Access to fisheries is an essential element of self-determination, which Winnemucca argues is limited by their inability to govern their waters "as at first," when their supplies were at their most abundant. Winnemucca thus calls for a reorganization of the Paiute body politic around the people's livelihood practices and not the arbitrary boundaries of settler policies.

Fishing had significant cross-cultural and intertribal benefits for the Northern Paiute economy. "The fish runs were occasions for festivals," Johnson explains, adding that "when the supply of fish was large enough a trout feast was held" in a celebration with "other basin tribes including the Washo and Shoshone" (1975: 9). These celebrations represented a system of intertribal, that is, inter*national* exchange which speaks to the complexity and sustainability of the Paiute economy. However, when settlers dammed up the river, reducing the flowage, they caused a massive decline in the production of fish and "deprived many of the reservation Paiutes of a source of income" (1883: 194). Winnemucca positions the Paiute nation as a mature body, possessing the knowledge necessary to raise healthy children who can thrive in this place. Trees and fish define the Paiute national body and root it in the storied relationships that Styers says are essential to decolonizing praxis.

Conclusion: From Tears to Landback

Toward the end of *Life*, Sarah receives back-to-back bad news about her people. The on-reservation school she started has been disbanded, and the Army is spreading false reports that her students never learned anything. The conditions at Yakima, where her people are being held, are abominable. The army is starving them and keeping their clothing rations. The man delivering this news to her sobs, tears running "down his cheeks," and "of course," Winnemucca explains, "I cried" (1883: 106). Sarah's heart is broken because of the constant losses and forced dependency on the US government. Just then, a liaison for the federal government Colonel Wilkinson walks up to her and thoughtlessly asks, "'what are you crying about?'" observing that Sarah is "'only an Indian woman'" and "'Indian women never cry'" (1883: 106).

Tears gain metonymic power throughout *Life* and when grieving the dispossession of Paiute people, they catalyze decolonization. In *The Cultural Politics of Emotion*, Sara Ahmed establishes the "stickiness" of textual signs, how they become "saturated with affect," making language ideal for initiating political action because language can "move us" both emotionally and physically (2004: 195). As they embody her grief, Sarah's tears stick to readers who too feel the traumatic wounds produced by separating Paiute people from their land. Once emotions are embodied, Ahmed acknowledges, that "it is up to us where we go with these feelings" (2004: 202).

Attentive listeners to Winnemucca's story now know and have possibly shared in the tears shed by many Paiute people. Winnemucca does not respond to Wilkinson, but instead directly addresses the readers: "Ah, my dear friends, he is another one who makes people believe he is working for Indians" (1883: 106). She underscores the great irony—and threat—of his words, considering this man works with multiple tribes. What can Sarah do? What can anyone *do*? *Life* ends on this note, with hot emotions and a raw wound. Below the text's final words, Winnemucca places her petition to Congress: a call to action for readers, now literate in their responsibilities to the land and its original children. Winnemucca's project seeks to motivate the collective action of conscientious friends to respond and embody the land lessons they have heard. Her petition describes Malheur as:

> [W]ell watered and timbered, and large enough to afford homes and support for them all, where they can enjoy lands in severalty without losing their tribal relations, so essential to their happiness and good character, and where their citizenship, implied in this distribution of land, will defend them from the encroachments of the white settlers.
>
> (1883: 108)

References in the petition to "timber" and "waters" operate with layers of metonymic force as they call to mind Sarah's storied memories of the land. They signal relationships with fishing and pine trees, which form a record of the

Paiute people as a mature, proud nation emblematic of Winnemucca's land-based decolonizing praxis.

Although the United States did not relinquish control of Malheur, Winnemucca's petition received thousands of signatures from enthusiastic supporters, as Elizabeth P. Peabody wrote to Lyman Abbott of the Christian Union (1886: 26). As Winnemucca's supporters copied and canvassed her words, they demonstrated an awareness that being together on the land was essential for preserving Paiute cultural identity and sovereignty. Signing and canvassing Winnemucca's petition translated the negative feelings readers might have felt into a productive outlet for decolonial action. The mindful and purpose-driven design of Winnemucca's decolonizing praxis brought some of her readers safely through the chaos so that they could react to the reflexive power of language with a critical understanding that, as occupying bodies, their actions must unsettle colonial power relationships. Such praxis demonstrates how decolonizing bodies is not merely about recording the traumatic wounds of colonization, but also about creatively unsettling through bodily practices like grieving, storytelling, and remembering the land, as manifested through Winnemucca's congressional petition, autobiography, and the voice of a sentimental child. These are all tools that colonizers typically use to exert control, but Winnemucca uses to heal such wounds by reconnecting Paiute bodies, knowledge, and traditions with the land.

Winnemucca's insistence that Paiute people remain on Paiute land connects her political project to ongoing landback justice movements. According to Eve Tuck (Unangax̂) and K. Wayne Yang, returning the land is an essential element of decolonization, which is not "swappable" with other justice movements because of the specific goals to unsettle colonial control (2018: 3). Decolonization, then, is about returning "everything that was stolen from the original peoples," including language, ceremony, food, education, housing, healthcare, governance, medicine, and kinship, as stated in one manifesto for the current #LANDBACK movement (2022: Landback). Winnemucca's petition, likewise, makes it clear that returning the land must be the first step, because it connects to "so essential to their happiness and good character" (1883: 108). (For other examples of the centrality of land to decolonization efforts, please see Part III of this volume.)

Although the aesthetics of the movement have shifted from sentimental appeals, like many of the Indigenous activists leading the movement today, Winnemucca creatively drew on the affective tools of her political moment to educate white Americans in the literacies of the land and engage them in decolonizing action. Such storied relationships with the land actively taught Winnemucca's nineteenth-century readers how to be stewards in a way that was not dominating and paternalistic, but rather willingly responsive to the needs of Indigenous communities. Winnemucca presented her argument for Paiute landback in lectures and performances across the country despite strong bouts of illness which, according to the editor's preface of *Life*, made speaking for long periods difficult. Like other activists working for liberation, she gave her body for her cause (see also Arani, this volume). Writing her autobiography relieved her body while enlisting white settlers in the labor necessary for unearthing deep-seeded colonial deposits.

The failures of existing social institutions to account for the labor of decolonization make nineteenth-century activist literature like Winnemucca's autobiography essential for understanding the archives of historical injustice. Her narrative contains an awareness that what happens to the land happens to our bodies and insists that it is the responsibility of all people to listen to and learn from these stories. This collaborative approach addresses the immediate challenges examined in Arani's and Higgins's essays (this volume) by modeling an inclusive and just reckoning with our shared history. The overwhelming action from Winnemucca's many supporters evinces the deep bodily impact of her land-based pedagogy and the ongoing power of Indigenous stories to fundamentally alter the way settlers live in communion with the land and its original stewards. Her life's work, then, stands as a prime example of how Indigenous writers at times of unadulterated land seizure and institutionalized erasure creatively use the affective tools of their cultural moment to tell good stories and make decolonial children of the land.

Bibliography

Ahmed, Sara. *The Cultural Politics of Emotion*. New York: Routledge, 2004.

Armstrong, Jeannette. "Land Speaking." In *Speaking for Generations: Native Writers on Writing*, edited by Simon Ortiz, 175–222. Tucson, AZ: University of Arizona Press, 1998.

Bruchac, Joseph. "Storytelling and Native American Writing." *Halcyon* 12 (1991): 35–41.

Cariou, Warren. "Terristory: Land and Language in the Indigenous Short Story—Oral and Written." *Commonwealth Essays and Studies* 42, no. 2 (2020): 39–48.

Carpenter, Cari M. "Choking Off That Angel Mother: Sarah Winnemucca Hopkins's Strategic Humor." *Studies in American Indian Literatures* 26, no. 3 (2014): 1–24.

Hermann, Ruth. *The Paiutes of Pyramid Lake; a Narrative Concerning a Western Nevada Indian Tribe*. San Jose, CA: Harlan-Young, 1972.

Johnson, Edward Charles. *Walker River Paiutes: A Tribal History*. Schurz, NV: Walker River Paiute Tribe, 1975.

Kimmerer, Robin Wall. *Braiding Sweetgrass: Indigenous Wisdom, Scientific Knowledge and the Teachings of Plants*. Minneapolis, MN: Milkweed, 2013.

LANDBACK. "Manifesto." *Landback*. landback.org/manifesto/ (accessed December 1, 2022).

Noble, Marianne. *The Masochistic Pleasures of Sentimental Literature*. Princeton, NJ: Princeton University Press, 2000.

Peabody, Elizabeth Palmer. "Sarah Winnemucca's Practical Solution of the Indian Problem a Letter to Dr. Lyman Abbot of the 'Christian Union.'" 1886. *Project Gutenberg*, July 17, 2018. www.gutenberg.org/files/57526/57526-h/57526-h.htm.

Powell, Malea. "Rhetorics of Survivance: How American Indians Use Writing." *College Composition and Communication* 53, no. 3 (2002): 396–434.

Samuels, Shirley. *The Culture of Sentiment: Race, Gender, and Sentimentality in Nineteenth-Century America*. Oxford: Oxford University Press, 1992.

Sanchez-Eppler, Karen. *Dependent States: The Child's Part in Nineteenth-Century American Culture*. Chicago, IL: University of Chicago Press, 2005.

Senier, Siobhan. *Voices of American Indian Assimilation and Resistance: Helen Hunt Jackson, Sarah Winnemucca, and Victoria Howard*. Norman, OK: University of Oklahoma Press, 2001.

Styres, Sandra. "Literacies of the Land: Decolonizing Narratives, Storying, and Literature." In *Indigenous and Decolonizing Studies in Education*, edited by Linda Tuhiwai Smith, Eve Tuck, and K. Wayne Yang, 24–37. New York: Routledge, 2019.

Trejo, Judy. "Coyote Tales: A Paiute Commentary." *The Journal of American Folklore* 87, no. 343 (1974): 66–71.

Tuck, Eve, and K. Wayne Yang, eds. *Toward What Justice? Describing Diverse Dreams of Justice in Education*. New York: Routledge, 2018.

Wewa, Wilson. *Legends of the Northern Paiute, as Told by Wilson Wewa*. Corvallis, OR: Oregon State University Press, 2017.

Wexler, Laura. *Tender Violence: Domestic Visions in an Age of U.S. Imperialism*. Chapel Hill, NC: University of North Carolina Press, 2000.

Winnemucca, Sarah [Hopkins]. *Life among the Piutes: Their Wrongs and Claims*. 1883. Monee, IL: Arcadia, 2017.

Chapter 5

EMBODYING AZADI: CONSCIOUS AND UNCONSCIOUS WOMANHOOD IN INDIAN OCCUPIED KASHMIR

Inshah Malik

This personal essay documents an intimate process of self-examination triggered by the 2019 annexation of Jammu & Kashmir through the removal of Article 370 of the Indian constitution by India's Modi-led government. Drawing on Carl Jung's analytical psychology as explored in his 1916 work on the psychology of the unconscious, I engage in an exploration of self by connecting it to the Kashmiri collective unconscious. Informed by *Sufism* (Islamic mysticism), *daleel wanen* (story-telling), *Zindagi hund tajrube* (lived experiences), and *Zindagi hinz dastan* (life narratives), I show how the collective unconscious of Kashmir holds embodied refusals and reclamations.

Exploring the "unconscious" offers insights into what Jung calls the common "bond of desire and longing." For Jung, these deep-rooted aspects of human nature connect individuals at a profound level, crafting a collective unconscious of humanity—containing memories, experiences, and symbols common to all humans across time and cultures. In this essay, I do not look at his work strictly from a psychological perspective, but my aim is to explore the notion of bodily refusals. What role does the unconscious play in reclaiming self-knowledge under cataclysmic political upheavals? Do such events induce "non-being" through undemocratic imperial statecraft, violent militarization, and extermination? What does "non-being" mean for a Kashmiri feminist political theorist rooted in such an inheritance?

Living far from Kashmir, I piece together memories triggered by the 2019 annexation. I grew up in the political community of downtown Srinagar, the heartland of rebellion against Indian rule. I explore my own self-construction through relaying and reviewing the lives of kin and community members who embodied, performed, and improvised womanhood. I reflect on my childhood and adolescence during different political periods, in different contexts, and intergenerationally, to explore how Kashmiri womanhood is entangled with the collective unconscious to reveal a site of decolonial praxis and knowledge generation. I review the inter-relational life of my mother (*Mae*), my maternal grandmother (*Bobe*), and especially my paternal grandmother (*Raje or Dadi*) as templates of womanhood in the Muslim matriarchal cultures of Kashmir. I also map manhood relationally, as depicted by encounters with men in my life—my father (*Abu*), brother (*Boi*), a medic (*Muzafer*), various counterinsurgents and Indian Army soldiers. As figures, each offers a relational understanding of self, morality, and virtue that shaped my character. Exploring these *daleels* (stories), I underscore both the violence of "nonbeing" and show how it is resisted through the dialectical experience of Kashmiri womanhood.

The Daleel *of the "Miracle" Birth*

The race against forgetting, subjection, and suffering makes the people of Kashmir keen storytellers. As a form of sense-making, storytelling is mired in a dialectical merging of the known and unknown. This merging accommodates the "loss of control" over life. The *daleel*, in a traditional Kashmiri sense, means a story that imparts moral lessons. The word *daleel* came into *Koshur* (Kashmiri) from Persian (in Persian/Arabic it means evidence or proof, but in Kashmiri, it means story). This traditional use of the *daleel* methodologically borrows from *Qassas-al Quran* (Stories of the Quran), making *daleel* an idiom of a Kashmiri mystic aesthetic. Unlike the English word story, *daleel* attempts to evoke a "narrative of truth." In its colloquial use, when asking a friend where they have been, we usually say, "*tse kya daleel, tse kati*" (what is your story, where have you been)?

In the 1980s, at the beginning of the armed conflict in Kashmir, in downtown Srinagar, everyone narrated their *daleel* as an assertion of bodily sovereignty. It intrinsically afforded ownership of our personhood. The instinct to have control over oneself through a *daleel* makes you unique, much like influencers on social media today (see Yahaya, this volume). *Mae* (mother) poetically narrated the *daleel* of my birth. I recall my excited voice, when I would ask her, *be kethpeath zaʾayas* (How did I come to be)? She would narrate how *Bobe* (my maternal grandmother) prayed specific tahjud (nightly prayers) asking for my birth. *Mae* was certain about her inability to conceive another child, as one of her explosively infected ovaries was removed through an emergency operation right after my brother's birth. Doctors told her to give up wishing for another child. She had to accept reality.

However, *Bobe* was relentless in her prayers, and to her doctor's surprise, *Mae* conceived. It was a miracle and proof that *Khoda* (God) answered the prayers of the pure ones. For *Mae,* my existence was proof enough of her faith. She repeated this *daleel* throughout my childhood, working it into a cohesive psychological bond between us. It was a sign that I was sought, desired, and wanted. As a relic of my desirability, this *daleel* contrasted with the reality of the political undesirability of Kashmiri bodies, who were being actively eliminated by military forces in our neighborhood lanes and also undermined the social preference for a male child. I realized the *daleel* of my miracle birth bore a metaphorical quality, offering hope in a desperate political turmoil.

Identity, Names, and Zaath

Abu (father) chose my name. He called me *Khansha* (an Arabic word that literally means snub-nosed)—an epithet for a gazelle, a metaphor for beauty. *Boi* (brother) called me *Daanish* (the Persian word for knowledge and wisdom). *Khansha* was shelved because people would conflate it with the *Koshur* word *khanun* (which means to dig). *Daanish* was shelved because it was a name for boys. After some discussion, *Inshah* (Arabic: to create, express, and write, modern Persian lexicon: an essay) was agreed upon by Mae and *Abu*. *Inshah* was a Koshur, Persian, and Arabic word, familiar to everyone in Kashmir, an amalgamation of cultures, accommodative, and reflective of our collective condition and our cosmopolitan past. In this condition of co-acceptance, there was no rupture between Arabic, Persian, or Kashmiri. My name was spoken in diverse pronunciations: *Bobe* would call out in a formal and respectful manner, *Inshahav*; our neighbor, *Noore*, who was the daughter of our milkman, would call me in a more personal, intimate, and endearing manner, *Inshae*.[1] There were other variations of my name, such as *Insa*, which I heard from an Indian army soldier stationed in the bunkers near our lane. The inability to pronounce the syllable "*sh*" bemused me. Whenever I treaded near the army bunkers stationed by our house, on looking out from a window, *Bobe* alerted me, *"ye chu panjaeb mintary wol"* (It's a Punjabi military man). Kashmir had historical trade relations with Punjab; to her, every outsider from the Indian plains was essentially a *Punjaeb*.

Bobe, *Child Marriage, and Intergenerational Trauma*

Bobe was a pious woman, a widow, and clad in a black *burke* (veil). She was a regular visitor to the Jamia Masjid, a historically significant central mosque in the city. Her deeply impressionable spirituality and the boundaries that she constructed for herself and by extension for me occasioned by asking probing questions. *Bobe*

---

1. During social-cultural interactions or space-sharing, caste or *zaath* is not generally explicitly discussed in Kashmir. But endogamy is still widely practiced, despite political and social movements, education, and increased awareness. While the politics of caste were reintroduced during Hindu imperialism since 1847 CE, they were preserved by Muslim nobility. The *Koshur* language has caste markers of this social inequality. The educated or clergy families (of all religious denominations) practice endogamy and contribute to the precariat of the masses, who are at various periods of the history freed from land labor.

was a strong supporter of the conservative Islamist politics of Mirwaiz Farooq Shah. *Mae* grew up as an orphan, without her father, in a family of four headed by *Bobe*. *Bobe* came from a wealthy family of *Mahingars* (traditional gold carvers). However, by the time *Bobe* reached her teenage years in the 1930s, her family had lost everything.

Bobe became a child bride to Ghulam Mohammad Mir (my deceased grandfather). At the age of sixteen, she was shown a picture of a young man and agreed to a *nikah* (marriage). On the day of her wedding, she felt embittered because she wasn't married to the man in the photo. Ghulam Ahmad Mir, her husband, was older, with two deceased wives and sons the same age or even older than *Bobe*. Hurt and anguished, she returned to her family. *Bobe's* father arranged for an *istamfaroush* (notary) to have her divorced. As *Bobe* vividly remembered this, her eyes welled up with the same anguish that this experience had caused her. She narrated how, on a fateful Thursday, she waited for Ghulam Mohammad. She had twisted and turned in anticipation the night before, and her eyes were fixed on the door, waiting for his arrival. She asked God (*Khoda*) to intervene and help her make the right decision. When he entered through the gate, she was moved by compassion. She empathized with him, felt the loss of his wives, his unhappiness, and loneliness. *Khoda* had chosen her to take care of this man. She called off the divorce and decided to return with Ghulam Ahmad Mir.

When I heard this story, I wasn't sure if her exceptional empathy and self-sacrifice in the face of injustice were an extension of helplessness rather than courage. Did consideration for her poor father inform her decision? She justified this situation through a moral metaphor: her sacrifice would please *Khoda*, as He is the disposer of all affairs and beholder of Justice. *Khoda* will ultimately book those who commit injustice and deceive others. When I heard this story as a child, it angered me. It sounded like fiction, a way to justify her decision to herself. Her choice to return to live with an old man did not make any sense to me. Growing up, I often pestered her, questioning her choice to return. As I revisit *Bobe's daleel* now, as a middle-aged woman, I become aware of the relational and circumstantial difficulties she must have experienced, how her navigation through calm piety and acceptance of her life circumstances symbolized love.

For *Mae*, *Bobe* was a helper and a caretaker. After work, *Mae* often took me to visit *Bobe*. On one occasion in early 1988, on a crowded bus, Mae stood holding me in her arms. A man who was seated offered to put me on his lap. We arrived at *Bobe's*, to a fun-filled day with cousins, toys, and treats. In the evening, upon our return home, I complained to Abu: "Are you a poor man? Why can't you afford a bus seat for me"? Mae realized I was uncomfortable about the incident on the bus. Crowded buses in Kashmir are not safe for women in general, and for children in particular, as prying sexual harassers find this an easy place to assault and escape. *Mae* equated my "hypersensitiveness" with *Bobe's*. My acute sensitivity to abusive words, touch, and my quickness to anger came from an unconscious inheritance of responding to injustice in the social milieu. While *Bobe* chose piety as a response, within such a culture of hierarchical social injustices, I confronted people, discarding traditional wisdom and challenging the status quo.

What Do We Want? Azadi *(Freedom)*

In the late 1980s, student politics and mobilizations signaled an intense political contest between the Islamist groups of the Muslim United Front (Bakre) and the nationalists of the National Conference Party (Sher). In the landmark elections of 1987, the mass political mobilizations pushing for larger democratization and self-determination took an ugly turn.

Seated on a *taakhshe* (embrasure) of a window, *mae* fed my toddler self bowls of rice mixed with saffron, sugar, and milk. I sat in the embrasure for hours, spotting birds that might be interested in competing with me for my rice pudding. The scenes of war, carrying the dead and the wounded might have crossed my path. Over the years, I have realized I have repressed painful memories. With *Abu* always away and working, *Mae* was dealing with uncertainty and the possible looming death of any one of us. At every turn, in our downtown Srinagar lanes, ambushes occurred and uncanny bunkers and checkpoints appeared. Meanwhile, *Mae* maintained strong ties of kinship, caring for less fortunate children in our extended family.

Unlike the general lack of interest or casual approval I saw from other children about our collectively inherited social world, I stretched and broke down the accepted norms. *Mae* was shocked by my questions that righteously sought logical explanations. At the age of five, I asked her the ominous question: if God created everything, then who created God? Her colorful imagination and faith couldn't engage my rational mind. Her life of service, frolic, emotion, and sensory experience was too difficult to touch with the preciseness of rationality.

In the 1990s, ghastly images of the dead in the newspaper, *Daily Aftab*, entered our house. I wonder now what symptoms of dysfunction appeared in me after seeing them. The pictures of mutilated dead bodies captioned with *Koshur* inscriptions form my memorabilia of the past. These memories appear as indicative currents rather than visual memories. I remember *Mae* concernedly speaking to our neighbors about my inability to sleep during those nights. Not much else comes to mind; perhaps *Mae* did a *phoukh*.[2] It is during those days that I first encountered the word *Azadi* (freedom), and it was the most desperate of cry of the people among whom I was raised, a slogan, wall graffiti, a plea.

Growing up during a raging armed struggle in the 1990s marred my own self-actualization. While at home, I spoke fluent and poetic Koshur; at school we spoke Urdu and English, both languages of imperial impositions. Our grandparents inherited Persian as a second language, a remnant of our medieval past, since it served as a lingua franca and a court language since Kashmir's Sultanate Muslim rule began in 1346 CE. Urdu, on the other hand, was introduced by the Dogra rulers of the Indian plains in 1846 CE, and English, though introduced by the

2. *Phoukh* is a ritual performed after praying Islamic prayers in Kashmir. After the prayer is complete, the prayer sayer turns to a loved one and blows on their face with pure breath. This is a ritualistic custom seen in Muslim cultures of Kashmir.

British imperialists, did not become a popular language until the 1990s. Naturally the question arose: if Indians and Pakistanis were fighting the British, what were Kashmiris doing? We only knew that we were fighting for our own freedom. In the Kashmir of the early 1990s, many Kashmiri languages were banned, while Urdu was promoted as a state language, and Hindi was spoken by the minority students of *Sikh or Pandit* (Hindu) backgrounds. Growing up in such a context meant that most of us struggled to make sense of who we were and felt a sense of loss, as we were less rooted than preceding generations in Kashmiri language(es) and culture. As a result, mapping the experiences of Indian rule over Kashmir can also be mapped through an intergenerational *daleel*.

At home, we were fully ourselves, but within administrative and institutional spaces, our identity was always contested. Are we Indians or Pakistanis? Do we have a more nuanced Central Asian past? What is our connection to the Slavs of Eastern Europe? Our schools avoided teaching the history, culture, or native language(s) of Kashmir. We were constantly making sense of ourselves through the prisms of the popular leaders of the independence movements of the Indian subcontinent. In our imagination, they were *nebre (*elsewhere or outside), in Delhi or Lahore. Our language is laden with markers that demarcate the boundaries of a nation: *panun* means our own, *wopar* means stranger, *kaeshir* means Kashmiri people, *kasheer* means Kashmir, *andar* means inside, *neber* means outside. The word for India was always Hindustan, and later *Hindustan te Pakistan*, referring to the great plains of Punjab and onward, Russia is *Rus*, China is *Cheen*, and Iran is *Eeran*.

Muzaffar: A Medic and a Bright Light

In April 1995, amid the heightened armed militancy and civilian movement restrictions, desperate *Abu*, with the help of a cousin, secured admission for me to the SMHS hospital burn ward. Upon arrival, I found myself in a special room resembling a personal office. A young man dressed in a white robe, with shining beautiful eyes, appeared. Muzaffer became my healer, tending to my burn wounds for the next twenty-seven days. I eagerly anticipated his daily morning visits at 8:00 a.m., where his bright presence, fragrance, and calm voice accompanied our one-hour wound-dressing sessions, gradually transforming them into a space of meaningful *daleels* (stories).

I was healing and curious to peek into a mirror. Muzaffer incorporated my curiosity into his *daleels*, carefully narrating the depths of my facial scars, areas filling up and those needing extra care. It was a comforting yet dreamlike experience, filling me with hope for a brighter future outside the hospital. His narratives spoke of Azadi (freedom), the blossoming of flowers, and the beauty of *novbahar* (new spring). It was April, typically spring in Kashmir, and his *daleels* served as a metaphor for hope, the promise of peace, and a dignified future.

Approaching the end of my treatment, I decided to satisfy my curiosity by hiding a spoon under my pillow, using it as a makeshift mirror to catch a glimpse of my reflection. My face appeared swollen and orange, leading to a moment of petrification and profuse tears. The next morning, Muzaffer spoke of my calmness. It was the first time someone had observed my development as an individual. As he dressed my wounds for the last time, he wished me luck and promised to be there the next morning to get me discharged.

The following morning, we waited, but Muzaffer did not come. My persistent inquiries revealed his absence. I wished to express gratitude and convey a desire to stay in touch. I later learned that he had offered his own office to be my ward in the absence of a children's burn injury ward at SMHS hospital. His sensitivity and psychological insight healed not only my burn wounds, but also my psychic scars. A few days later, *Abu* delivered the shocking news that Muzaffer had died in an ambush with the Indian army. The revelation left us all in surprise and uncertainty. Was this gentle physician also a militant, part of a network of Kashmiri men fighting the Indian state? Or just caught in the crossfire? We would never know.

Coming of Age, Witnessing, and Scarring

In our household, regular conversation about the ghastly horrors, tyrannies, and oppressions of ordinary people by various militarized forces, particularly by counterinsurgents, abounded. The newspapers, radio stations, and television sets relayed nonstop reminders of our collective subjection. A war was raging in the streets, men were *mujahid,*[3] *shahid,*[4] and *begonah*[5] and women were spoken of in hushed tones, as *behurmati*[6] and *roisiyahi.*[7]

By 1993, our home in the downtown Srinagar neighborhood of *Khankah Moulla* was an epicenter of war. Curfews and crackdowns were used as counterinsurgent tactics to suppress the popular armed rebellion. Every "crackdown" (cordon and search operation) in our neighborhood caused *Bobe* emotional distress. She would send my uncle, who was endearingly called *Papa*, to check on us. During this time, *Abu* had started a business to provide a better level of education for my brother. *Boi* was admitted into one of the top-ranking schools for boys, Burn Hall School, a remarkable feat. My uncle insisted that *Mae* move into the maternal house, because it was unsafe for her to raise us, as Abu was often away, and Indian army soldiers had a free hand in entering our homes at will, in search of militants. We moved to the maternal house, closer to *Bobe*. This helped *Mae* continue working since *Bobe* could watch us. In those years between 1993 and 1998, our family grappled with many difficulties, including poverty and Abu's absence.

3. The one who strives for truth (in Islamic context a religious truth but in Kashmiri context a political truth).
4. A martyr who is a witness.
5. Someone not guilty of crime, especially crimes against humanity or the state.
6. Dishonor.
7. To be left black-faced in dishonor.

Still, *azadi* or freedom had a strong imprint in our subconscious. Experiencing and witnessing the intense desperation for political freedom, I learned the most bitter lesson about my existence: to be free is to not be without rights, to be without rights is the state of being Kashmiri, to be Kashmiri is to be weak, to be weak is to be a woman, to be a woman is to be emotionally fragile. These subconscious messages made me distance myself from my mother's emotional world, a world crafted through patience, tolerance, acceptance, and living through immense difficulties. I anxiously internalized a political reality of living and growing up under a patriarchal military occupation, a world crafted through an endless lack of freedoms.

The Counterinsurgents

We returned to our home in *Khankah* in 1998. I had begun going through puberty during yet another difficult phase of the armed conflict. As I turned sixteen, the Indian state was containing the popular armed struggle through the use of counterinsurgency forces. Even walking on the streets was unsafe, yet I walked from my home, in the heart of downtown Srinagar, to various locales where teachers offered private tuition. Private tuitions compensated for missing regular school days due to government-imposed curfews and strikes called by pro-freedom leaders to resist participating in public life. Under those circumstances, neither buses nor roads were safe. Gun-wielding men on motorbikes called *Naabid*[8] abounded; they were informal counterinsurgent groups of Kashmiri men who chose to surrender and assist the Indian state in curbing the popular armed uprising.

My first encounter with a *Naabid* and my own coming of age are mired in unusual circumstances peculiar to downtown life. For many months, I walked from my home in *Khankah Moulla* to *Zaine Kadel* where I would meet my friend *Asra*. From her house, we walked across *Zaine Kadel* toward our chemistry tutor's house in *Karan Nagar*. For months, an AK47-wielding *Naabid* followed us, in order to start a relationship with Asra. She was clearly as terrified as me. After many months of tolerating his harassing behavior, which included holding our paths, passing sexist comments, and terrifying us in a very local hooligan style, I finally had enough of him. Without letting Asra have any inkling of my intentions, one day, as he began casting sexual innuendos at Asra and circled us on his bike, I became furious to the point that I almost blacked out. Losing control, I shouted at him to the point that the shopkeepers in our locality, who had barely ever dared to speak to him and his gang, felt encouraged to support us. His gang of *Naabid*, sensing the collective anger rising, began to disperse, but he did not retreat without first threatening to kill me if he saw me again. I returned home shaking and terrified, resolved to never leave home again.

---

8. They derived the name from the place of their origin in a village called Nawabidipour in Bandepour district.

The next morning, I woke up but couldn't muster any courage to get ready for tuitions. *Boi* noticed my unease. As I got out of bed to greet him, he came up to me, looked sternly in my eyes and said, "You have to go, if you die, I will be proud of you, but you can't stay home." Later on in life, the memory of his intervention exemplified to me an alternative world of freedom that was possible through the friendship of men. His intervention at such an early age testified that the lack of freedom in our social and political world could only be tackled by becoming fearlessly free ourselves. When I think about what encouraged him to instill such fearlessness in me then, I could only think of one fearless woman who had perhaps subconsciously impacted him too.

Dadi, *Memories, and Resistance*

Our paternal grandmother, Raje Begum, affectionately known as *Dadi*, was a matriarch. Despite standing at a modest 162 cm, her presence exuded strength and self-respect. She wasn't someone who simply received commands; rather, her mere presence effortlessly commanded the respect of those around her. She was vocal and walked with a quiet confidence, as if untouched by the travails of life, despite having had her fair share. Unlike *Mae,* who adhered to a strict routine, *Dadi* floated through her days. Her life was marked by leisure, song, poetry, and gardening. She impressed upon me the importance of fighting for a place in this world by embracing vulnerability.

Dadi's spirituality relied on Kashmiri Sufi poetic traditions. She profoundly impacted my personality development in ways I am conscious of, and I have reflected upon her exemplary life and teachings throughout my own life, both consciously and unconsciously. These reflections have helped me in reassessing, healing, and addressing my own traumas and difficulties. I felt a deep belonging with Dadi. As one of her youngest grandchildren, I frequently found myself in her presence. Out of all her grandchildren, I was more often called *Rajenzur*—a term used to signify a granddaughter who closely inherits her grandmother's traits.

My fondest memories with *Dadi* are centered on her *braand* (balcony). Culturally, *braand* serves as a station to behold Kashmir's scenic beauty, where one can witness the snowfall in winter or the cheerful chirping of birds in spring. Women clean vegetables, sort rice and grains, or sit leisurely, sunbathing by lifting up their trousers to the knees. They engage children in feeding their proverbial curiosity about nature, life, and the mysteries of the world. It is here that *Dadi* narrated delightful *daleels* and fed me bowls of rice mixed with lamb soup. In these moments, she drew my attention to the chirping of the *tsare* (sparrows), *Kantar* (hoopoes) and *Bulbuls* and let me take in the fragrance of her garden's *golab (roses)*, and at night, engaged me in gazing at the *zoon* (moon) and *tarakh* (stars).

The primary theme of her *daleels* was morality, and her method of narration evoked in us an ability to discern good from bad. *Dadi's* spirituality was unshakable, revolving around *tawheed* (monotheism), praxis, and service. Her narrations about Mir Seyed Ali Hamdani, a Central Asian Islamic mystic of the Kubraviya Sufi order, followed by life *daleels* of Kashmiri mystics, *darvaishs*, or *reshis,* such as Hamza Makhdoom, Sheikh Noorudin Wali, or Nund Reshi, Sheikh Hanifudin Reshi, Sheikh Hamza Maqdoom, and Lale Ded (most of whom are either Brahmans or were formerly Kashmiri Brahmin convert to Islam), and their later successors such as Soch Kral, Wahab Khar, and Ahad Zargar shaped a syncretic, monotheistic mystical tradition where these figures were claimed by Kashmiris, despite their apparent religious identity.

Dadi supported her five children by spinning pashmina threads, which she would sell to shawl weavers. Through this enterprising activity, she managed to educate all her children, who went on to serve in different sectors of Kashmir's economy. *Dadi* deeply valued education; she would always advise us to learn. Owing to her enthusiasm, it was always a question for us: how did she not receive formal school education? All of us, her grandchildren, often knew her answer verbatim. She had repeated the story to each of us so many times, with so much anguish, that it had become our collective anguish.

In 1931, impromptu mass protests erupted in support of Abdul Qadeer, a rebel seeking rights for Kashmir's Muslims. His trial became a landmark political event. His fiery speech at *Khankah Moulla* Shrine, the center of Kashmiri Islam, marked a turning point against the Dogra regime. Sheikh Abdullah, a Kashmiri nationalist leader, emerged at the helm of this national uprising against the Dogra regime. Since the early twentieth century, Sheikh Abdullah and groups of Kashmiri Muslims had invested in a massive mobilization for education. From all downtown locales, children were taken away to be enrolled in government schools to receive primary education. These schools were notoriously called *Zabri Zaet* (forced humiliation) since most parents were unwilling to send their children away and were satisfied for them to only have religious education. *Dadi's* poor parents hid her from government officials and informed them that they "didn't have any daughter," which is how she missed getting enrolled in the school. Her parents later justified their decision by asking, "In her absence, who would wash the dishes?" The anguish on her face and the grief seeping through her words always felt deeply personal to me. It was an anecdote of grave injustice meted out to her, and she fought throughout her life to undo the harm that a lack of education did.

Nearing ninety years of age, she retained around 3000 Kashmiri *beaths* and poems. Her marital life was not a prominent subject in her anecdotes; she briefly mentioned her husband, Mohi-ud-din Malik, describing his physical appearance, gentle character, his long battle with tuberculosis, and early death. The details of her marriage remained obscure, leaving room for speculation on the dynamics of strong matriarchal women in successful intimate relationships. She embodied Kashmiri nationalism, and was exposed to politics through speeches Sheikh gave at *mimbers* (mosque pulpits) and *Jaloos* (public gatherings), which offered her an opportunity to learn. However, her cousin's killing by the Dogra police forces during the 1931 protests—whose grave lies in the martyr's graveyard in *Khoje*

Bazar in the courtyard of *Astan Naqshband*⁹—offered her real insight. She learned firsthand about the oppressive nature of the Dogra regime. The denial of basic freedoms and the repressive politics of containment of dissent inflicted trauma. She resolved to keep the memories of her experience alive.

During cold winter nights, she would gather her grandchildren around and recount *daleels* about the conduct of Dogra police forces, who, upon entering market spaces, demanded that people bow and kneel in respect. Noncompliance resulted in flogging. The people of Kashmir were restricted in practicing their Islamic faith, as Dogra rulers imposed Hindu customary laws. For instance, the consumption of beef was criminalized, despite the fact that even among native Kashmiri Pandits, meat-eating was an accepted dietary practice. The fear of consuming beef was deeply rooted in the community psyche, particularly for *Dadi*, to the extent that she prevented us from eating it. Even when legal restrictions on beef-eating were not enforced in the 1980s, Abu, who was fond of it, consumed it in secret.

Dadi's concept of *azadi* (freedom) encompassed the freedom to practice her faith, the right to education, the right to land and resources, and the ability to cultivate a political consciousness. In the 1990s, she believed many of those freedoms were won; however, the question of the right to self-determination was stymied. Due to her struggles, the right to education was granted to me, and my parents became upwardly mobile, middle-class individuals with substantial social networks. However, *Dadi* did not anticipate a massive armed uprising against the Indian state. In the new Kashmir, I had no right to disagree with our political system, militarism, or politicians. The political system that replaced the Dogra regime had successfully evaded the question of Kashmiri political will—a politics about which *Dadi* was acutely aware. There were no free or fair elections; one could not disagree with subcontinental politics by rejecting the "two-nation" theory that had partitioned India and Pakistan. I could not situate my own history, languages, culture, or knowledge in this newly inherited system.

She was particular about her five-time obligatory *nemaz* (prayer), and yet, her spirituality had a strong social and cultural angle as well. I could only piece together an understanding of it many years after she passed on, when, at a wedding ceremony in Kashmir, I saw her sister. As I entered the venue, she signaled for me to come close and whispered, "Are you *sakhav* like *Raje (dadi)*"? The Kashmiri word *sakhav* is used for someone who is generous, a helper, or a healer in the community. This reminder about my grandmother's character brought back many memories. I recall people coming to her with *hajat* (needs). When someone expressed financial needs, she simply signaled for the person to sit close to her,

9. A sufi shrine built by Soltan Sikander in 1389 for Baha-al-Din Naqshbandi, founder of Naqshbandi Sufi order where one of his descendants Mohi-ud-din Naqshbandi is buried. Sufi Shrines in twelveth-century Kashmir played a pivotal role in the cultural, linguistic, and spiritual propagation of Islamic mysticism in Kashmir.

and when no one was looking, asked him or her to take the money from her *pheran* (Kashmiri traditional tunic) pocket—a gesture she would make so as not to embarrass her borrowers. The social and cultural aspect of her personality as a healer, helper, and a leader centralizes the psychotherapeutic value of Sufi spiritual practice. She offered safe spaces for grief and grievances. Her leadership, guidance, and counsel were sought after not only by her children, but also by the community of extended family, relatives, neighbors, and friends. Her *mashvare* (consultation) centralized the needs of those who asked and tailored solutions that resolved the underlying issue. Her interventions respected the boundaries of those who sought her help; she never discussed things told to her in private. Her resolutions often revolved around the words *darguzar karun* (forgiveness), *pardeh karun* (hiding others' limitations), and *khodayas afu mangun* (seeking God's forgiveness).

In the 1980s, when new Islamist movements emanating from Pakistan made their way into Kashmir through discourses predominantly published in Urdu, she continued to practice her own understanding of Islamic mysticism. In 1996, *Mae* was sprayed with color by extremists, in order to force her to wear a long Indian/Pakistani-style burka. *Dadi* was visibly upset. She had worn a Kashmiri *burke* modeled around the Afghan burka all her life, but this new wave of Islamism smacked of cultural imperialism. New Islamist women intervened in cultural politics, teaching Islam in Urdu as the medium of instruction and employing materials emanating from Pakistan. Veiling was adopted, not only to allow for public and cultural inclusion of women, but also to resist the neoliberal Hindu cultural homogenization propagated by the Indian state's imperialism.

Before her passing, I had the honor of meeting *Dadi* one last time. She appeared frail and something moved me to inquire about my grandfather. She repeated the anecdote, "Your grandfather was a handsome man; he was everyone's favorite." She paused briefly, and I sensed that was all she intended to say. Lifting her frail body, she leaned in toward my ear, ensuring no one else was listening, and continued, "But he always made me feel inadequate." Her admission exposed the deep-seated trauma she had carried within her. It prompted me to reflect on how Kashmiri women, for generations, have forged robust personalities despite their lack of political, social, and individual *Azadi* (freedom), and how these traumas permeate into intergenerational experiences and legacies.

Conclusion

As I make sense of my own unconscious inheritance in this essay, *Mae* and *Bobe* provided a blueprint for how to lead from the heart, and that by accommodating, accepting diversity, and leaving room for error and forgiveness, one could live a dignified and disciplined life. *Dadi* impressed upon me the need to fight against injustice through her memorization and narrations; she centered remembrance as an important motif. Her approach sought to prevent normalizing injustice by passing on the memory of trauma caused by subjugation to Dogra rule or the difficulties of navigating an interpersonal relationship with her husband.

Many of her teachings that live in my unconscious guide my own interventions into the political world that I have inherited. This deep-rooted understanding of a Kashmiri Islamic mystic's life has involved a self-reflexive view of my own self-formation, a view complicated by a tumultuous political history. The more I bring this unconscious mystical life that was impressed upon me into consciousness, the more I understand the nature of the unfreedoms women and men continue to experience in our part of the world. Just as *Dadi*'s personality had developed through grappling with a plethora of unfreedoms, her active struggles made possible my own intellectual life. Through the stories of how the rights of women are easily deprioritized, such as the story of how her parents preferred her to wash dishes instead of going to school, she was cautioning me all along. She had planted the idea that brutal authoritarian regimes should not be respected when she narrated stories of her participation in protests against Dogra rule.

Early on, her stories pushed me to actively dedicate my life to writing about Kashmir and its politics. I became one of the first women in my family to travel abroad to receive an international education. If she had witnessed the kind of education I have gotten, perhaps it would have soothed her, and maybe she would have wanted a similar level of education for herself. However, it would have pained her to know that life for an educated Kashmiri woman was not necessarily much better in terms of their freedoms. Educated women and men like myself live through an on-and-off war, face the risk of extermination, curbs, restrictions, removal of rights, and exile, in addition to grappling with a fast changing social and cultural milieu that imposes imperial social and cultural practices and accentuates materialism to displace Indigenous cultural bonds and networks. In this milieu, Kashmiri womanhood emerges as a site of decolonial praxis and knowledge generation, through the intergenerational traumas and resilience within matriarchal Muslim cultures. Kashmiri women have for generations crafted robust personalities from their lack of political, social, and individual *azadi* (freedom). These traumas are intergenerational and inform the agency and personal development of Kashmiri women like myself.

Chapter 6

FRAGMENTS CONTAIN WORLDS: ENCOUNTERS BETWEEN NARRATIVE PRACTICE AND FILMMAKING

Xiaolu Wang and Poh Lin Lee

Introduction

In late 2021, Xiaolu reached out to Poh to request narrative practice consultation in relation to an ongoing film project. Poh offers conversations to filmmakers by centering their lived experience in the co-research[1] (Epston and White 1992; Epston 1999, 2014) of practice, ethics, and political engagement. Narrative therapy brings together different ideas and practices, informed by cross-disciplinary exchange and contributions from fields like feminism(s), decolonial theory and praxis, social justice frameworks, social anthropology, philosophy, literary theory, and educational psychology. Narrative therapy means different things depending on the practitioner, the site of practice, and the discursive context. Many practitioners actively call this "narrative practice" in order to establish it outside the sole claims of the professionally regulated therapeutic industry. What distinguishes it from traditional therapeutic models is that it centers deconstruction, power, context, and intersectionality. At its heart, it is an approach informed by the voices and experiences of those at the center of conversations.

In this piece, we exchange two bodies of practice—filmmaking and narrative practice. We invite you to stay with us in the fragments of experience and encounters between bodies. In that *mélange* of the not-yet-known, emerging meaning-making process, we simultaneously speak to and experience decolonial ways of coming to our practices. We construct a relational collaboration outside of traditional client/therapist structures by positioning this practice as two-way and collective (Carolina Caycedo et al. 2019). We resist the colonial insistence on a specific type of movement—as filmmaker, to successfully complete a film at all costs—and as "therapist" to lead clients in a direction deemed desirable and rational (Lee and Vaswani-Bye 2022).

---

1. Co-research marks a shift from empathy to ethnography to discern that rather than researching "the person" or "the other" we, as practitioners, could join with people as co-researchers of their experience and accompany in meaning making endeavors.

From the outset, we release ourselves from the expectation to discern the therapeutic from the creative. We both share the unbearable weight of demands to be, perform, think, feel, and imagine in certain ways in order to be granted access, acceptance, support, and status from our respective industries of practice. We discern between our specific industries and fields/communities and identify the former as systems and institutions formed in the image of colonial ambitions that snake out into complex patterns impinging on bodies and movements.

In this piece, we look together at intentional decolonial practices like attending to place, pace, rhythm, the centering of metaphor, and the invitation to *body community* to participate on their own terms. By "body community" we do not see the body as a single entity or story, but rather as a diverse community of different members, each with their own relationships, histories, positions, and experiences (Lee 2023). This decolonial perspective on the body actively resists individualism and the forced disappearance of collective and community accompaniment and participation. We resist extractive ways of engaging with lived experience and story (Murrey and Mollett 2023) and refuse to co-opt body participation for outcome and productivity (Federici 2020). As we unpack our shared conversations in this book section dedicated to decolonizing collectives, bodily refusals and reclamations, we hope you, as the reader, experience the possibility of giving value or visibility to bodily practices, relationships, and acts that you are imagining or are already a part of.

Collaborative safety emerges from honoring the integrity of the shape and form of each body of practice so that we might be attentive to the moment-by-moment exchange: "we exist, not as wholly singular, autonomous beings, nor completely merged, but in a fluctuating space in between" (Mia Birdsong 2020: 19). We use "we" when we are going somewhere together, not necessarily with a destination in mind. We honor safe conditions first in order to get lost. We are curious about what we notice in the landscape when we get lost in it. In *Open Door*, Rebecca Solnit (2005) describes getting lost as a process of letting the unfamiliar appear. Our conversations offer a similar experience of disorientation. We are interested in what could emerge from choosing indeterminate movement and determined togetherness. These conversations nourish our bodies outside of dominant structures. We need each other to unlearn and move in unexpected ways.

During our conversations, Xiaolu noticed how Poh's practice spoke to their own curiosity for the less familiar. This resonated with Xiaolu's desire to depart from extractive filmmaking practices and formulaic ways of being. In order to unpack and slow down the perpetual striving in life and in filmmaking practice, Xiaolu felt the need to make space for unlearning (MTL Collective 2022). Poh and Xiaolu recorded three dedicated conversations as part of this process and in this chapter share three fragments from these recordings in a multilayered unpacking.[2]

---

2. While we are interested in challenging ideas of therapy done clinically behind closed doors, it is not with full ease and simplicity that we choose to share these video fragments of private conversation. We connect with Mardiya Siba Yahaya's comment on the complexity and risk "In this way as well, our bodies become searchable, accessible and usable from a distance in a timeless manner" (Existing Beyond Time and Place: Understanding Queer Muslim Visibilities Online).

Poh
Do you recall what was happening at the time that you requested we meet?

Xiaolu

In April 2018, I opened an email about the film *An Elephant Sitting Still*. The email was sent by a film organization that no longer exists. I remember one line in the email that drew my attention: Hu Bo (the director) took his own life soon after finishing *An Elephant Sitting Still*. Glancing over the email, I remember pausing and getting curious about the reasons he ended his life, but the demands of my daily life filled the pause immediately. I never looked up what happened to him.

About a year later, the film was presented at the international film festival in the city where I lived. I vaguely remembered that I had come across this film before. What followed was an intense and mysterious rabbit hole in which I read the original short story that the director wrote and looked up anything I could find out about the suicide. I watched the film on the silver screen, with sparse audiences in a small theater. The film programmer apologized at the beginning that the film was about four hours long. I thought that was the most disrespectful introduction to a work ever, especially when the filmmaker is not alive to defend his own work. Indeed, some people complained during the screening and stormed out. I was the only person standing up and applauding with warm tears running down my face when the credits rolled through. At the end, there appeared a black-and-white photo of Hu Bo, with a statement that the copyright of the film belongs to his parents. This statement cost one's life to secure.

Between 2018 and 2019, I was also in the generative creative phase of making my first short film. I was well under the spell of the "hero's journey" (Taylor 2022). At that time, it seemed as if I was being supported in reclaiming my own lived experiences as an immigrant child, but the available tools I had access to actually reproduced the colonial gaze. Dutifully, I declared a vision and gathered community and resources around the project. I was set to prove myself as a filmmaker, as having something worthwhile to express.

These days, I have been questioning uncritical visions that give shape to process and community. Because of my dissatisfaction with myopic visions that already exist in the world, I procrastinate on articulating a vision. I would say I am in the process of defining a vision, a voice, my own flavor of the creative process, loosening old patterns of productivity, creativity, and what success looks like. In this process, I found myself in a community of artists departing from a colonial way of filmmaking who also want to drop out more, play more, experiment more, risk more, fight more, rest more, dig more, question more, and get lost more.

The death of the young director impacted my mental health and my desire to produce work. My creative stagnation is intricately tied to this death. It was not just one artist's decision to end his life, it was not just one tragedy. Instead, it was the failure of an industry, a community that includes you when you are willing to play the game, but excludes and blames the individual when you refuse. I identified with Hu's story and his refusal to compromise. The tragedy signaled a lack of options. It reveals to me the working conditions of artists and filmmakers within a system that disregards the possibility of remaining true to oneself, to experimentation, and to a sense of dignity.

Encountering you, Poh, and redefining ways of working is changing the game for me. Your questions and presence, by asking "What members of the body are supportive?" or "What parts of the body are not in agreement?" make visible the complexity of communities, within and outside of the body, how we are accompanied by many presences, conflicting desires, and contradictions, and are not always in accordance within ourselves, and how the internal pressure and struggle are not any less important than external forces. My body was exhausted from the posturing and performativity required to play the game. What are my options besides exiting? Your questions opened up new possibilities within the body and imagination for a different way of being.

Before I renamed the project *Wet Togetherness*, I was making an entirely different film—a portrait documentary of an unorthodox synchronized swimming team taking the sports world by surprise. But I never felt like "I" was making the film at all. The industry and the conventions of the documentary world had me by my throat. I couldn't feel my voice at all. Any trace of a voice. I went to documentary labs and workshops, only to be more entrenched within the hero's journey and dominant modes of production. I wrote and won a production grant that supported the gaze of the hero's journey and left me alone with the task of reconciling with members of my body who were in disagreement. What I continue to discover and experience is that bodies are always honest, and I was too separated from it to hear the signs.

Then 2020 happened. I had fallen out with almost the entire film community where I had worked since 2018. I suppose that I was finally exhausted by the regurgitation of ideas and repetitive image-making. I was alone, in a society of spectacles, which even a global pandemic couldn't disrupt. I didn't turn away this time. I surrendered to the couch, to rest, and to be with a solitude named "getting lost."

It would have been a missed connection with Poh had I stayed on course with the hero's journey. In this sense, I am ever grateful for getting lost and losing control. A new relationship with knowledge is emerging. A different sense of knowing is forming. In 2021, this sense of knowing was affirmed by a particular space to which I brought the film. I started to meet artists, coming from different contexts and different parts of the world, who are more grounded in their practices and full of similar doubts and questions about documentary practices. A politics of listening was possible and a language of critiquing the hero's journey continues to expand. As I surrendered to the richness of disorientation and loss, and noticed the strengthening of intuition and sensibility, that's when I met you, Poh, along with this new film title and description.

Wet Togetherness

The spirit of a drowned child leads Xiaolu on a pilgrimage to dismantle the fear of water. By visiting with humans and marine mammals who are exploring interdependence and collective organizing, new paradigms emerge, of engaging with the water and each other.

Inviting witness
We invite you to position yourself as a witness to our conversation. Here are some possible questions to accompany you while witnessing:
– Which expressions or images stayed with you in particular ways? Why?
– What are you encountering in your current practice that made you curious to get involved in the exchange between Xiaolu and Poh?
– Are there colonial unlearnings that you are also a part of?

Xiaolu

Dear Poh, at the time of our conversation, I seemed to not know how to locate myself and describe my positionality. I don't know where I am, where I am moving, or where I want to go. I am now writing from Amsterdam, a place where I have my bearings for at least a week. At the time of the conversation, I had no idea where to move toward. There were too many possibilities, yet none at the same time. How I came to be in Amsterdam now has something to do with the relationships that materialized as I carried the same questions and confusions. Maybe the excitement of meeting people I've yet to know and love got me to where I am now. I got accepted to a fellowship with a cohort of film critics, programmers, and filmmakers for a year. Through this very international cohort, I met a fellow

scan here
Fragment 1: Locating oneself in relationship with the project through metaphor

https://vimeo.com/802688513/3fa4b074bd

filmmaker who lives in Amsterdam. There is sunshine coming from the window. We are sitting in her living room as I type out this paragraph. The new snow and the desert I was speaking of in the metaphor seem far and foreign now. But that aloneness is still familiar.

Poh

Dear Xiaolu, when you shared that you "didn't know where you are" in our video fragment, I was accompanied by an idea that even if we don't know where we are, we are still somewhere. These days, how do we know where we are? Is it based on maps, roads, fences? What if we try to locate where we are through relationships? What about where we are in relationship with more-than-human[3] figures? I heard you speak about wishing to be in relationship with a body of water. Where does one body end and another begin? What is the space in between? The intermingling? What kinds of relationships do we have, or can we have with bodies of water? I heard you discern where you were as no-longer-desert, nor yet-with-water.

之间[4] *In-Betweenness*

This connects each of us to our familiarity with the in-between, in life, in practice, in identity, shifting from seeing this place as a barren, no person's land to one with flourishing communities and ecosystems. If you care to slow down, whole worlds are collectively revived.

Poh

When I meet with a filmmaker, like I did with you, I do not see that I am meeting an individual body even if physically they appear alone. From my perspective there are already multiple figures in the conversation, but for now let's say there are at least two bodies—the filmmaker and the project. This already influences my positioning in the practice. I am interested in the relationship between the

---

3. "More-than-human" invites us to step away from colonial practices of designating all that is not human to a lesser rank on the hierarchical ladder. By using it here it is a political act of re-valuing and challenging discourses that perpetuate othering. This enables people in conversation to include treasured members of diverse communities that would otherwise be dismissed or overlooked. "The absolute distinction between the natural and the human that is so central to Western ways of thinking leaves no room for other-than-human beings to figure as protagonists in history or politics; at best, they can be treated as inert elements in particular ecological settings" (Ghosh 2021: 58). "Even without decentering the human by narrating the world from the perspective of nonhumans, storytelling about human experiences with other-than-humans has the potential to change today's world" (Fenske and Norkunas 2017: 105).

4. 间 is a character with the "sun" in the middle surrounded by an open "door." This character carries the meaning of "in-between," "intervals," "moment," "room/the smallest unit." "之" is a shape-shifting character, which only has meaning in relation to other characters. It could signify location, possession, and position.

filmmaker and the project as this invites a relational way of unpacking position, beliefs, ideas, actions, and experience. It also means that there is the possibility of collective responses to the concerns that the filmmaker might be encountering or up against. This does not mean that the filmmakers themselves experience a collective presence. Rather, filmmakers often speak about the effects of industry-led individualization of practice and process, positioning the burden of labor and success/outcome expectations heavily on their bodies and identities. But it does have a significant influence on the types of questions that I may ask and that I resist asking. I'm interested in questions that explicitly counter individualization, privatization, and commodification of creative practice/process. These types of questions reposition creative practices and processes firmly back within the socio-political-spiritual context and refuse to adhere to divisions between art making/therapeutic practice/social change and collective rites of passage.

At the beginning of our first conversation (just before the first video fragment begins) you described *"I feel this metaphor for swimming with this whole project is, I think I am learning what it means to get in (the water) … I think Wet Togetherness is formed, it feels like it's learned to stand on its feet … now we're probably getting ready to plunge in."*
I got interested in whether there were dominant ideas that were demanding that you and I see "getting in the water" as the first step. What does this exclude? I was also curious whether "getting into the water" as an intention for the project could also somehow be under the spell of linear expectations of process and story. What might the relationship be between "getting into the water" and ideas of outcome or success?
As we continue to move within the metaphor, I notice how you chose to place specific fragments of your context and experience into the metaphor. I notice how this significantly resists the idea that the practitioner needs to "know all the details of a person's life or experience before they can engage." Through metaphor I witnessed you actively choose, select, and share what you would like and I can receive this within the simultaneously clear and mysterious metaphor—the active process of being seen on one's own terms and in one's own expressions. It makes me wonder what would have happened if we had taken a more expected approach of starting with "fear of drowning" or "difficulty in learning to swim."
I imagine it could have invited well-circulated ideas of problem-solving, management, and "overcoming" personal weaknesses/blocks, and I wonder how these might shape a certain way of *coming at* our bodies. By engaging bodily refusal of these dominant helping/saving/solving approaches we instead hear, you describe *"It feels like I'm under some kind of spell, like, I cannot swim. And then, I'm like, I guess searching for something else that would just like, break that spell."*

When I ask multiple questions, I do not mean to direct this at you expecting that you respond to every question. It is a scaffolding where I am attempting to convey multi-directional possibilities, tentatively and collectively. For me, it's like placing these multiple questions into the shared range (Gumbs 2020) between us rather than aiming them across into/onto your body. By placing them in the shared range between us, we can both look at them together, shuffle, sift through, and sweep some aside until you notice a theme of questions that are generative for you.

In my early twenties, I encountered the practice of exoticizing the domestic (White 2004: vii) in narrative practice that proposes a counter practice to modern rationality that *"... obscures, diminishes and marginalizes diversity in modes of life and thought. As a consequence of this, people's lives are rendered routine and, in a great many circumstances, sub-ordinary."* At the same time I was also reading Haruki Murakami's book *The Hard-Boiled Wonderland and the End of the World*. I got curious about the relationship between narrative practices and the political life of magical realism that seeks to interrupt colonial constructs that dictate what we give value to, how we relate to time, truth, history, and where we place our attention.

Murakami has a way of loitering[5] with the most mundane activity or description and establishes a very specific pace and rhythm. And this, for me, weaves a spell. I'm reading endless descriptions that lull me into a certain tension, threading the spell .... and then .... I literally miss the moment where we've entered another dimension. Suddenly there we are and the transport is done in such a way that we seamlessly cross over to this other worldliness. Single truth-seeking gatekeepers dissolve. I'm listening closely for the mundane descriptions that often get sped up or skipped over for the dominant narrative arc at play, the one that has us convinced of the need or value to get to the key point of the story, or the most difficult part, or the moment of truth. I'm interested in revaluing or centering the mundane as a threshold or doorway into worlds of infinite possibilities, co-breathing spaciousness in and around our bodies.

时间[6]+空间[7] *Spaciousness*

We attend to valuing spaciousness, collaborating with spaciousness, and requesting a relationship *with* spaciousness. In the first video fragment, Poh asks multiple small questions that in other contexts may be overlooked or dismissed in the rush to get to the "essence." This attention to spaciousness at the beginning of our conversation creates the fertile ground for unlikely connections between

---

5. Michael White (2007) encouraged us to "loiter with intent" in narrative practice conversations. See also Ross Gay's essay on loitering (2019) and Phadke, Khan and Ranade (2011).

6. 时间 is translated as "time" in English, but "时" is "time," and "间" is "room or space," so the Hanzi characters for time, contain both time and space, they are not separate notions.

7. 空间 is translated as "space", and Xiaolu finds it interesting that "space" contains the word "empty" in Hanzi, space is a form of nothingness, and it is rich in its emptiness.

experience and meaning. Spaciousness joins us in countering expectations, the need to get it right and other stifling discourses that benefit from restricting movement and breath. We participate in spaciousness. The idea is distributed frequently that space is, as a resource, limited, finite, and therefore restricted to privileged access. This connects us with Silvia Federici's words, "Fixation in space and time has been one of the most elementary and persistent techniques capitalism has used to take hold of the body … Mobility is a threat when not pursued for the sake of work, as it circulates knowledge, experiences, struggles" (2020: 121).

Now, we invite you to take a look at the second fragment of our shared conversations.

scan here

Fragment 2: Inviting our multi-storied body practices in our co-research

https://vimeo.com/802688926/e9b5866ec6

The practice of considering our bodies as multi-storied invites us to actively re-call community presence and participation by imagining, in conversation and exchange, that our bodies are not single entities but instead thriving communities (Lee 2023). By communities, people have named and described exchanges with and between community members like Bones, Heart, Viruses, Spirit, Head, Intellect, Toes, Shoulder, Chest, Top half and Bottom Half, Intuition, Fatty Tissue, hosting other and Beings, Blood, Jaw, Eyes, Bacteria, Muscle, Energy, Breath, (multiple) Voices.

Poh

In this fragment and in response to your sharing I wondered—would there be members of the body community who might be prepared or interested to participate and collaborate in this search together?

These invitational practices have emerged through my experience of responding to trauma and displacement in many contexts including family and domestic violence, state-sanctioned violence, and forced migration. Questions are my craft and passion—I deeply enjoy the practice of shaping questions that are response-based, deconstructive, invitational, political, and relational with the intention to accompany people in their many endeavors to articulate and share experience. This is one way I actively choose to notice, discern, and shift my practice from extractive ethics in the ongoing movement toward a co-creative space. I witness daily the profound effects of what happens when someone has articulated an experience in ways that they haven't before, or crossed a threshold into finding language for the not-yet-said. I witness the movement toward reclaiming inclusive story-making rights and rituals.

"What has the spell convinced the breath of?" I asked around 0:51 of the second video fragment. I realize as I look back at this moment that this question is familiar to me on account of externalizing within narrative practice. Externalizing is a playful, political deconstructive practice that foregrounds the relationship between the person and the experience rather than misidentifying the person as the experience (White 2007). I see how I rested on the assumption that it is clear—that somehow I had conveyed all of that in my question—but I really hadn't! Awkwardly, I watched myself repeat the question slowly until finally I caught up that I'm not being more clear by repeating the same words and then adding more words. Noticing this and finding ways to come back alongside you is my labor and if I do not take this up I risk sitting comfortably in my position whilst leaving you at risk of possibly experiencing a sense of failure or not having enough (of something) to participate fully in the question.

Xiaolu

You asked, "What members of the body have been most affected by the spell?" At 0:51 of the second fragment, I immediately answered, "breath." Breathing is a basic instinct and right to life, but we don't even think about breathing until it is threatened. The struggle to swim emphasizes the access to breath. Breath is carried a certain way when the body is not allowed rest, relaxation, and a calm nervous system regulation. I wonder how much the way I breathe is similar or dissimilar to my grandmother's patterns of breathing.

A friend taught me about this failure to imagine one's need to breathe while her respiratory system was affected by air pollution in Northern Thailand. We were in the same environment, but my body didn't show many signs of protest. My friend developed a sore throat right away, while I didn't give much thought to breathing. I felt for my friend, but I also couldn't feel what she was going through. This dissonance happens when we are only listening to our individual experiences and dismissing the air that is affecting us on a collective level.

呼吸[8] *Breathe*

How on earth do you get anyone to believe that your breath is under a spell? How do you even describe how breath can be stopped or captured by pollution, discourse, or historical experiences? And more pressingly, how is it affecting all of us?

I have never considered my body as a host site of community, a meeting of different desires, wills, capacities, and preferences, because I am trained to assert the "I" as a tangible cohesive individual. I breathe for myself alone. When I say that my breath is affected by a spell, it is a spell that is reinforced by this myth of the individual.

Poh

直觉[9] *Intuition*

I noticed you named *intuition* in our shared conversation. With this word comes so much about how I *should know* what this means.
In this moment of writing it shows its form to me as a collection of knowledges[10] that we might sometimes term body knowledge, ancestral knowledge, collective knowledge. Because they are deemed mysterious in terms of their form, location, or source, they are subjected to distrust and their values are diminished. I can get hooked into trying to define which knowledge *it is,* as if the source, form, and validity must be "knowable." I get distracted into locating the truth of the knowledge rather than listening quietly to its offering and the chance to be in quiet conversation with multiple knowings even when they contradict each other. I welcome the mysterious forms of knowledges that move through and around me, you and us, and refuse to categorize.
This is the first time I hear you talk about a near-drowning experience. I'm grateful to you for conveying to me the significance of our co-research during this moment and in relation to the project and lived experience. Accompanied by knowledge and practices co-produced with people and communities responding to displacement/injustice/trauma, I wished to position myself in ways that would invite multi-storied accounts of this particular experience so that we could both acknowledge its seriousness but not in ways that overshadowed the particular precious knowledges, responses, and relationships that made it possible for you to have survived.
As you were responding, I was accompanied by ideas and practices centering on community and collective responses. I was cautioned by these bodies of

---

8. 呼吸: Breathing is the cycle of exhaling "呼" before inhaling "吸".

9. 直觉: intuition. "直" means straightforward, "觉" is "senses." Xiaolu finds that "straightforward feelings" is close to the expression of "gut feelings."

10. This has us traveling to Inshah Malik's insight about how our bodies produce meaning in the contexts they inhabit, and contexts give meaning to the bodies, our knowledge therefore is contextually embedded as well (Embodying Azadi, this volume).

know-how and wisdom to ensure that my questions did not individualize your experience. My hope was to ask questions that might make these community members not only visible but present and fully able to participate in the conversation as much as each one wished.

Making community visible in practice -
a movement from individual thinking to body community

The noise! As I attempt to ease into non-linear meandering movement.   a place of uncertainty, liminality.   a collection of selves of various timescapes.   Being with these moments of not knowing, not holding a direction or outcome.   Listening with body   blah blah blah blah I write when I find myself in the space in between.   The place of forming the not-yet-known, not-yet-seen, not-yet-said.   Quiet, silence, not absence of presence.   I'm not at ease in these moments of writing blah blah blah.   What if nothing comes back?   What if "I" is alone?

They are quietly steadfastly watching me.

Community of flesh and breath, posture and liquids

they are watching me,

checking the listening.   Will she succumb to demands to use her power over us and come at us as she's been taught so comprehensively to do. vision can get warped in ways that I turn on them head full of noise I start to imagine them as enemy or singular and failing or too strange I'm instructed to hide them.   I try to modify them.   they be Body Spirit Flesh Intuition Earth Community Bone … somewhere between all.   I shed the position I've taken up way out over here, the singularity of "I."

Close the distance—join place with them.

We invite you to take a look at the third fragment of our shared conversations…

scan here

Fragment 3: Presence of the Hero's journey

https://vimeo.com/802687130/63d4f2ea31

Xiaolu

It's hard to know where to begin with the indoctrination of the "hero's journey." I've heard it in artist talks, in relation to Joseph Campbell's books, and in graphs and charts that are made to illustrate milestones, significant events, breakthroughs, and the call to adventure that transforms the hero on their journey. This idea is always reinforced, validated as knowledge, as the voice of reason and authority. It's not a surprise that it is often linked to self-help endeavors. It begins with a goal on a linear trajectory. If you acquire more resources and skills under the pressure of finite time, you will be validated as an expert figure who gained insights to master maximum productivity. But what about the texture of lived experiences that grow sideways instead of forward or upward?

In the name of emotional intelligence training, I ended up in a program, prompted by a mentor and desperation for transformation. When I speak of the "strange groups I've joined" around 14:40 of the third video fragment, this is the experience and context to which I am referring. In the style of a retreat, a room of about eighty participants from all over the United States was cut off from familiar routines and social identities for four days, to adopt a set of rules from the program and sign a waiver to signify that this is a choice on the part of the participant. What followed inside this program couldn't illustrate the dominance of the hero's journey more precisely. The program was broken into two modules called "Discovery" and "Breakthrough." Through exercises, role plays, games, and sharing, our task was to explore how we make decisions and choices in our lives without acknowledging our cultural backgrounds, geography, politics, or the intersectionality of our experiences. Many ideas from film, literature, pop culture, and Buddhism were extracted and co-opted to support the curriculum. Color-blindness was upheld as neutrality, and neutrality was the core philosophy that glued everything together. To maintain neutrality is to choose the higher power.

Some of the exercises surely provided new insights, but as I was going through this isolated and immersive experience in order to rebirth as a new version of myself, a persistent cough accompanied me. It would send loud signals to my body and sometimes force me to step out of the room. In fact, I was singled out by the coach as demonstrating a lack of self-care to be in the program. I was constantly reminded of who held the position of power in the room, and any tendency to quit was seen as a sign of not showing up with greatness. Participants are reinforced with the idea that not finishing the program is a reflection of a life-long pattern of giving up. And giving up is only a sign of failure, of untapped potential, and unrealized ambitions.

As Poh asked me some questions I found myself describing how my cough was taking care of me by disrupting the pressure to participate in expected ways. My breath voiced itself when other members of my body were busy maintaining order and obeying. Without obedience, you won't get the results you say you want. Without conformity, you are not a team player. Self-exploitation is disguised as self-enrichment, with the promise of achieving greatness if you are willing to pursue it at any cost. The day I finally quit the program, I took a shower after removing myself from all communications. The water was cleansing my body and spirit. I felt grateful for this moment because returning to my body and breath brought a sense of relief, along with a sense of knowing that I didn't abandon myself this time.

In the video fragment, I realized this obsession with "transformation" and "breakthroughs" that I have been chasing after has been controlling my desires all my life. Even this moment of realization fits into the life-long addiction to breakthroughs. There is no knowledge gained if there is no transformation. I see my ways of coming to filmmaking as being in thrall to the spell of the hero's journey; my efforts are measured by a very particular and singular way of being/doing/creating. Not only in how I am supposed to construct the story or chase after stories of triumph and overcoming, but also in industry structures designed to shape me into becoming a certain type of filmmaker.

I described to Poh this voice that is pushed down my throat. It demands that if I am learning to swim, I should dare to go deeper. The same thing shows up in the relationship to filmmaking: If I have a vision, I ought to give up everything for it to come to fruition. If I shift positions and question this vision or pause during the process, I must not be giving it all I could. That's why the act of floating doesn't follow the hero's logic.

Poh and I rolled these questions between us—what if the journey is multi-directional and together we resist linear movement forward? What if it's about having a relationship with water, to play and dance with the water, to enjoy floating on its surface? Poh then asked me, "What is getting in the way of celebrating floating, enjoying, and savoring the experience with water?" I realize that what is getting in the way is this habit of pretending and performing ambitions that are not my own. I have been trying on someone else's voice for a long time, but the smallest disruptions are never too late. In this refusal, I am learning to experience joy and ease as a decolonial practice.[11]

Months later, I came across a passage from a Daoist book of meditations. The words were so precise and almost identical. It affirmed again the multi-directional possibilities I'm curious to be in a closer relationship with.

Sailing 渡

Infinite expanse, sleek ocean teeming with life,
Turbulent, virile, ever-moving spread,
Seamlessly laid to the brilliant sky,
I float on you in my fashioned womb,
Sustained against your green-black depths.

---

11. We connect with Mika Lior's in depth exploration of pleasure as a resource and productive mode. ("Ele gosta do samba resguardo" ("He likes a rough samba"): Ceremonial embodiments of Bahian Candomblé Caboclo).

Those on land never understand maritime life.
Those of the sea are intimate with your moods;
They navigate but are ultimately helpless.
Destinations become useless, drifting the sole reality:
A sailor's fears dissolve into acceptance.

Tao is sometimes compared to the ocean. Its depth is immeasurable, and its power rules all who enter it. We seek to sail it with our knowledge of knots, direction, mathematics, and charts, yet our understanding is incomparable to its vastness. The young have great ambitions about exploring both above and below the surface, while the old have given in: They know that there is no other alternative than to accept the ocean and float upon it. One who accepts is sustained. Those who go beyond its terms meet death. Thus the wise say that they float here and there without care; they trust in the overwhelming power of Tao.

(From 365 Tao: Daily Meditations,
Sailing of March 22nd according to the Northern Hemisphere calendar)

ABOUT THE AUTHORS

Xiaolu

Dear Poh, my ancestors are made of grandmothers, orphans, the unborn, wounded warriors, bound feet, arranged marriages, soy milk and fried bread, egg-filled pancakes, the desert, Taoist teachings, Arabic chants I know nothing about, the Yellow River, the Helan Mountains, Mongolian and Uyghur blood, goji berries and dates, the white cloth that wrapped around my grandmother's bones, mosques, squares, oases, camels, bighead carps, and roots in the Ningxia Muslim Autonomous Region of Northwest China. I find intimacy in loss, shadows, memory, the fear of water and the awe of water, the stone's softness, the ineffable, poetry, mourning diaries, films, essays, reflections, and the courage to remain a small yet useful animal. In this life, I am dancing and chanting my way from entangled codependence and alienated self-reliance to wayfinding in interdependence.

Poh

Dear Xiaolu, I was speaking to Aunty on Saturday and we were remembering— her mother, my grandmother—Ah Ma's dedication to health and care through practices of gathering, preparing, and cooking food. In Australia, if I took a trip I'd often get asked questions on arrival, such as "How was your flight? Was it on time? Did all your luggage arrive?" My memories of arriving in Penang to see my grandparents were quite different. Ah Ma would greet us at the airport armed with flasks and thermoses and little packets of food. My parents loved to tease her for trying to feed us immediately on arrival. As a kid, I understood Ah Ma's practices of welcome as a kind of fear that we hadn't eaten enough and her suspicion about the nutrients we were receiving in Australia. But in conversation with Aunty I understood it differently. The foods Ah Ma chose to prepare were specifically crafted to take care of the toll of flying and traveling on our bodies. She would prepare cooling and grounding foods like mustard greens and sweet potato cooked in soup and then drained to only drink the clear liquid.

Remembering the taste of care while writing, remembering Ah Ma's care.

ACKNOWLEDGMENTS
Radhika, Shvetal, Gabrielle, Martine, Hannah, Iva, Rini

Bibliography

Allen, Irma Kinga. "Thinking with a Feminist Political Ecology of Air-and-Breathing-Bodies." *Body & Society* 26, no. 2 (2020): 79–105. https://doi.org/10.1177/135703 4X19900526.

Birsong, Mia. *How We Show Up: Reclaiming Family, Friendship and Community.* New York: Hachette Go Books, 2020.

Caycedo, Carolina, Marina Magalhaes, Carolina S. Sarmiento, and Jose Richard Aviles. 2019. "Decolonizing Space, Place and Body." *YouTube.* Uploaded by USC Price. 2019. https://www.youtube.com/watch?v=fbrSuiPUfiQ (accessed April 24, 2023).

Epston, David. "Co-Research: The Making of an Alternative Knowledge." In *Narrative Therapy and Community Work: A Conference Collection*, 137–57. South Australia: Dulwich Centre Publications, 1999.

Epston, David. "Ethnography, Co-Research and Insider Knowledges." *International Journal of Narrative Therapy & Community Work* 1 (2014): 65–8. Ethnography_co-research_and_insider-knowledges.pdf.

Epston, David, and Michael White. "Consulting Your Consultants: The Documentation of Alternative Knowledges." In *Experience, Contradiction, Narrative and Imagination: Selected Papers of David Epstein and Michael White 1989–1991*, edited by David Epstein and Michael White, 11–26. South Australia: Dulwich Centre Publications, 1992.

Federici, Silvia. *Beyond the Periphery of the Skin: Rethinking, Remaking and Reclaiming the Body in Contemporary Capitalism.* Ontario: Kairos Publishing, 2020.

Fenske, Michaela, and Norkunas Martha. "Experiencing the More-than-Human World." *Narrative Culture* 4, no. 2 (Fall, 2017): 105–10.

Gay, Ross (Guest). "On the Insistence of Joy." In *On Being. On Being Studios.* June 13, 2024.https://soundcloud.com/onbeing/loitering-by-ross-gay.

Ghosh, Amitav. *The Nutmeg's Curse: Parables for a Planet in Crisis.* Chicago: University of Chicago Press, 2021.

Gumbs, Alexis Pauline. *Undrowned: Black Feminist Lessons from Marine Mammals.* California: AK Press, 2020.

Lee, Poh Lin. "Our Bodies as Multi-Storied Communities: Ethics & Practice Fragments." *Journal of Systemic Therapies* 42, no. 2 (2023): 1–21.

Lee, Poh Lin, and Akansha Vaswani-Bye. *Co-Researching Anti-Oppressive Practices.* Workshop notes. Workshop for the Mental Health Institute for Washington State providers, Social Justice and Inclusion Training Track, 2022. https://uwspiritlab.org/training/mental-health-institute/sji-2/.

MTL Collective. "Principles for Decolonial Film." *World Records* 4 (2022): 81–2. https://wrjournal.wpengine.com/wp-content/uploads/2022/03/Vol4_Art7_Principles.pdf.

Murrey, Amber, and Sharlene Mollett. "Extraction Is Not a Metaphor: Decolonial and Black Geographies against the Gendered and Embodied Violence of Extractive Logics." *Transactions of the Institute of British Geographers* 00, no. 1–20 (2023): 1–20. https://doi.org/10.1111/tran.12610.

Phadke, Shilpa, Sameera Khan, and Shilpa Ranade. *Why Loiter? Women and Risk on Mumbai Streets*. New Delhi: Penguin Viking Books, 2011.

Solnit, Rebecca. *A Field Guide to Getting Lost*. New York: Penguin Viking Books, 2005.

Taylor, Stayci. "Queering Heroes' Journey." *YouTube*. Uploaded by The Evolution of Story. 2022. https://www.youtube.com/watch?v=_rtt_VXvVMc (accessed April 24, 2023).

Watkins, Mary. *Mutual Accompaniment and the Creation of the Commons*. London: Yale University Press; 1st edition, 2019.

White, Michael. *Maps of Narrative Practice*. New York: Norton, 2007.

White, Michael, and Dulwich Centre. *Narrative Practice and Exotic Lives: Resurrecting Diversity in Everyday Life*. South Australia: Dulwich Centre Publications, 2004.

Part III

SOVEREIGNTIES, AUTONOMIES, LIBERATION

Figure 4 Sowing Seeds by Bhasha Chakrabarti (2018).

Chapter 7

"ELE GOSTA DO SAMBA RASGADO" ("HE LIKES A ROUGH SAMBA"): CEREMONIAL EMBODIMENTS OF BAHIAN CANDOMBLÉ CABOCLO

Mika Lillit Lior

Ilê Axé Oba Ina Candomblé house, São Caetano, Salvador, Bahia, Brazil: *By the time visitors from neighboring ritual houses arrive, the* Caboclo *guardians of the evening's festivities have already embodied their devotees and begun dancing to a lively beat. A rowdy cowboy circles with a broad-shouldered, senior 'daughter of the saints' and extends a hand towards another elder initiate—a gesture of invitation to samba.*[1] *The elder accepts, maintaining her poise as the herdsmen or* Boiadeiro *gently draws her into an intimate, quick-paced and seemingly effortless samba duet full of breaks and accented isolations of the torso and hips* (fieldnotes, August 20, 2019).

The Caboclos are hybrid gods associated with Brazil's Indigenous peoples, and with mixed-race Afro-Indigenous field workers from Bahia's colonial and postcolonial past and present. Generally masculine-identified and often unruly, they are cultivated by women, men, and nonbinary gendered initiates of Candomblé, a syncretic African Diasporic religion established by enslaved and free Afro-descendent actors brought to Brazil through the transatlantic slave trade.[2]

I wish to acknowledge my teachers in Brazil whose support made this work possible, my intellectual and spiritual guides, and the lands where these dances and writings have transpired. This essay is dedicated to Mãe Oba who crossed the threshold in October 2021. Ruth Landes Memorial Fund and Fulbright-Hays Foundation helped realize the fieldwork involved in this research.

1. "Circling with" and "in," ("rodar com" and "no santo,") are the most common terms for divine embodiment in Bahia (see Lior 2021, 2022; Rabelo 2014). Initiates gain the title "daughter" or "son of the saints" when ritually reborn into the temple community or "familia de santo" (family of the saints). While some practitioners in Southern Brazil prefer the term "familia de axé," based on the Yoruba-Atlantic concept of *axé*, the "power to make things happen" (Thompson 1984), I embrace the "saints" because they reflect the language of my interlocutors across regional and ethnic affiliations in Bahia.

2. See Prandi (2001), Teles dos Santos (1995), and Brazeal (2003) for further historizations of Caboclo in Candomblé. On relations between Caboclo and Orixá, see Rabelo and Aragão (2018).

Rooted in West and Central African cosmologies, Candomblé also integrates influences from popular Catholicism, Amerindian medicine ways, Spiritism and Semetic knowledge systems.

Seen as insurrectionary and degenerative to European, Christian codes of decency, Afro-religious manifestations were policed under Bahia's Portuguese colonial administration, from the 16th to 19th centuries. In 1808, Brazil became the seat of the Portuguese Empire, with a constitutional monarchy that proclaimed Catholic Christianity the dominant religion and forbid the erection of non-Catholic places of worship. Despite these obstacles, around 1830, three priestesses of West African origin founded the *Casa Branca de Engenho Velho*, widely recognized as the first temple of Afro-Bahian religion (Butler 2001: 140; Castillo 2017; Cici interview Aug. 2018). To this day, across myriad ritual compounds, devotees of Candomblé invoke and embody a diversity of ancestral and divine relations through codified and improvised liturgies, rhythms, and choreographies.

Based on ethnography, history, and performance research in Bahia, Northeastern Brazil, this essay addresses Candomblé's ritual embodiments as loci of knowledge production and as resilient world-making social practices. Whereas ethnographers have largely focused on Candomblé's African-oriented *Orixá* practices in the most renowned temples of Salvador, Bahia's capital, my research foregrounds outlying temples, such as Ilê Axé Oba Ina, depicted in the above vignette, and their homages to the Caboclo legions. Unlike Orixás, whose praises are sung in Yoruba and who each perform their own symbolic choreographies but do not engage in social behaviors such as gossiping or drinking, Caboclos speak and sing in Brazilian Portuguese, tease participants, enjoy alcoholic beverages, and invite onlookers to dance in participatory samba *rodas* or circles. Developed by Africans on Bahia's colonial plantations, *samba de roda*, or samba in the wheel, mirrors the circular structures of Candomblé ceremony and involves solo and partner dancing accompanied by call and response lyrics and percussion.

In ritual contexts, devotees of Bahian Candomblé summon their Caboclo guardians with invocation songs and codified steps, proceeding in a circle that moves counterclockwise around the sanctuary. However, when the Caboclos arrive and take human form, they dance energetic, weighted sambas and sing narrative choruses that animate the room. Expanding on theorizations of samba outside of ritual contexts,[3] I suggest that practitioners of Candomblé's Caboclo mobilize samba dance and music to disrupt and reorganize enduring colonial formations that limit the movements, representational possibilities and bodily sovereignty of Afro-Bahian citizens. Caboclos' sambas thus constitute a fertile site

3. Natasha Pravaz's (2013) examination of the imbricated issues of cultural authenticity and sexuality among samba dancers in Rio's carnaval, informs my argument. Similarly, Cristina Rosa's (2015) investigation of samba's Africanist aesthetics, including polycentrism and polyrhythm, provides a foundation for my movement analysis. I also draw on Alberto Filho's (1999) historical account of post-abolition Bahia, in which samba street performance became criminalized as part of urban hygiene campaigns that targeted poor Black women.

for thinking, together with contributors to Part II of this anthology, about how embodied practices inhere political potential and advance the project of building decolonial futures. I ask, how do Caboclos' performances refuse the production of colonial and postcolonial power geometries? Furthermore, how do Caboclos articulate their own moral ideologies as they remake selves and reclaim space, bodies, and lifeworlds through private and public ceremonies?

To answer, I draw on insights gleaned from dance and ritual study in Bahia, especially under the tutelage of high priestess Mãe Oba, who enfolded me progressively over several years into the social fabric of her heterodox Candomblé, Ilê Axé Oba Ina. Helping with household duties before, during, and after ceremonies, I glimpsed devotees' extraordinary relational dynamics as well as everyday realities of economic marginalization and race and gender-based oppression. In addition to preparing the temple for ceremony, I also participated in ritual dances, adopting choreography as a theorizing practice and method of analysis (Shea Murphy 2007; Banerji 2019). As an overarching score that evidences a theory of embodiment and resonates with other systems of representation (Foster 1998; 2003), choreography defines acts of making meaning through dance. Extending performance researcher Christina Rosa's (2015) work on Afro-Brazilian movement patterns and the ways of knowing that they subsume, I identify the aesthetics of loose (*solto*) and broken or brokenness (*quebradinha*) as tactics that Caboclos and those who circle with them use to assert cultural and corporeal agency.

A matrilineal and matriarchal Candomblé whose Caboclo ceremonies valorize feminine discourses of pleasure, desire, and authority, Ilê Axé Oba Ina is governed by high priestess Mãe Oba, in memoriam, together with her successor and great-granddaughter Obá Kesojú and daughter Yá Oberekan, who holds the office of *mãe pequena*, right-hand to the priestess. Generations of women devotees in Mãe Oba's ritual family, from elders to young adults, embody their Caboclo here. During festive ceremonies and private offerings, the tones of the songs, dances and social interactions situate erotic play between female-bodied mediums and other initiates of the temple within Bahia's Afro-religious universe. Like the storytelling traditions embodied by generations of women in Inshah Malik's piece in Part II, their Caboclo dances and sung verses comprise living sites of everyday feminist praxes of bodily and cultural reclamation.[4]

Another series of festivals at Ilê Axé Oba Ina similarly include performances with erotic overtones, namely those dedicated to the urban tricksters known as Brazilian *Exu* and *Exua*. However, these Exu/a homages are held in the street—a space conceptually marked as appropriate for encounters that critically play on sexual metaphors.[5] Caboclos, in contrast, engage pleasure and desire within the temple sanctuary. Doing so, they carve out alternative sites that not only loosen and upset orthodoxies of gender and sex, but actively reimagine these norms, by attributing ritual and social value to performances of desire and desirability.

4. See the editors' "Introduction."

5. Similarly to the Orixá Exu, the Brazilian Exu and Exua govern the arenas of sex and money.

Figure 5 Caboclo Festa with three Boiadeiros at Ilê Omin Guiam, Itaparica, Bahia. August 2018. Photograph by Zendo Gedye.

Emerging as critical performance practices in Bahia's Candomblé houses, Caboclos' loose and broken sambas embody individual and collective autonomy and subvert (by virtue of shaking off and breaking down) Brazil's race, gender, sex, and class hierarchies steeped in colonial labor relations. Oral histories of Afro-religious genesis in Bahia, in addition to literary accounts, and statistical analyses (Teles dos Santos 2006) assert that Afro-descendent women have traditionally dominated Candomblé's leadership and mediumship ranks.[6] Embodying male-identified Caboclo beings, women mediums deploy stylistically masculine sambas as they forge their own authorial discourses to contest seignorial models of Black femininity based in Brazil's legacy of plantation paternalism and queer heteronormative gender dynamics of samba dancing. This essay thus situates

6. My interviews with practitioners of diverse ages and ethnic affiliations revealed broad consensus about the lead role of Afro-descendent women in Candomblé's nineteenth-century institutionalization, and about the enduring female centricity of Afro-Bahian ritual enclaves (Cici de Oxalá, August, 2018, Fonseca, May, 2018, Barbosa, May 2018). See Lior 2021 for further discussion of these findings. In their historical studies, Cheryl Sterling (2010) and Kim Butler (2012) address the predominance of women in nineteenth- and twentieth-century Candomblé. Scholars including Barbara Browning (1995), Paul Christopher Johnson (2002), Lisa Castillo (2017), and Jose Reis (2001) also contribute nuanced perspectives to debates about gender roles in Brazil's Afro-religious universe.

voiced and danced adulations of hybrid, under-theorized entities, the Caboclos, as creative lexicons through which Candomblé's primarily (though by no means exclusively) female practitioners respond to the ongoing, subtle, and direct effects of systemic sexism and racism rooted in Brazil's colonial beginnings.

Caboclos of Bahian Independence

Strategically situated on the Bay of All Saints, Salvador da Bahia operated as Brazil's colonial capital until the Portuguese administration relocated to Rio de Janeiro in 1763. During the transatlantic slave trade era, Brazil received more African bondspersons than any other nation, around five million. Between the sixteenth and nineteenth centuries, more enslaved Africans passed through Bahia than through any other New World port, with the sole exception of Rio de Janeiro (Ribeiro 2008), forming the foundations of Brazil's plantation economies.[7]

In Bahia's cosmopolitan sphere, Africans and Brazilians of African descent mingled with Amerindian inhabitants, Portuguese seafarers, and plantation owners. Devotional imagery and occult practices related to Iberian saints, Islamic religion brought to Brazil by Yoruban Muslims and Indigenous Brazilian and African traditions circulated among Bahia's racially diverse subjects. Candomblé emerged within this intercultural matrix as practitioners grappled with New World conditions of racial terror, patriarchy, and Brazil's Catholic colonial rule, under which Afro-religious manifestations were unevenly suppressed.

Though Brazil proclaimed independence in 1822, Bahian territory remained contested until Portuguese troops were finally expelled on July 2, 1823, making Bahia the last province to join the nascent Empire. Beginning in 1826, commemorations of Independence Day in Bahia featured a feathered "índio," a Caboclo statue, as a central figure of parades through the capital city of Salvador. Aiming a spear at the serpent dragon atop of which he stands, the Caboclo figuratively slays the Portuguese colonial tyrant. Another statue, a Cabocla, was added several years later. Cultural and neighborhood groups including military corporations and religious brother and sisterhoods accompany the Caboclos, singing, dancing samba, and revering them (Albuquerque 2022).

During the early postcolonial period, government officials supported the parading of the statue as an emblem of Brazilian identity that linked patriotic

---

7. Indigenous nations including Tupi language groups populated most of Brazil's Atlantic coastline when Portuguese settlers arrived in the early 1500s. Colonists depended on Indigenous forced labor until the first waves of African bondspersons arrived in the mid-sixteenth century and began working on sugar plantations. Sugar cane was the colony's primary export until the 1600s (Schwartz 2009).

freedom and anti-colonial sentiment in the public imaginary. Possibly, state representatives regarded Independence Day commemorations featuring the adorned Caboclo statues as commensurate with Christian displays of devotion because of their resemblance to popular Catholic saint processions.[8] Hence even though the new constitution only sanctioned non-Catholic religious practice in private (Gynn 1894), Caboclo Candomblés could take advantage of Independence Day celebrations to venerate their Caboclos as "local divinities" in full public view.[9]

Enshrined as a symbol of the nation's decolonial triumph, the Caboclo statue also accrued salient associations to Black enfranchisement. Toward the closing of the 1800s, slave owners distributed manumission cards promising legal freedom to enslaved Afro-Bahians during the July 2 parades. With the momentum of the abolition movement growing, vocal abolitionists also increased their presence on the event's civic stages. After Brazil officially ended slavery in 1888, the Caboclo statues gained starring roles in abolition day festivities as well.

While Bahia's colonial society revolved around the nucleus of the patriarchal family, located within the confines of the master house, during the post-abolition period, politicians and physicians became concerned with the ordination of public spaces and sought to "modernize" the "black city" of Salvador, along the lines of European cosmopolitan centers of the time (Filho 1999: 242). Because of samba's pelvic articulations, exemplified by the *umbigada* in which dancers thrust their hips toward each other so that their belly-buttons "bump," elites viewed the dances as inflammatory and obscene. These changing perceptions prompted turn-of-the-century urban reformers to question the appropriateness of samba in the Independence Day demonstrations.[10]

In the 1910s, these critiques coincided with calls to remove the Caboclo from Independence Day processions. Swayed by evolutionist ideologies, some literati

8. See Albuquerque 1999, pp. 74–5, 89.

9. Glynn, George A. (1894). *Constitution of Empire of Brazil*: "The apostolic Roman Catholic religion shall continue to be the religion of the Empire. All other religions shall be permitted with their domestic or private worship in buildings destined therefor [sic], but without any exterior form of a temple" (72). While the Caboclos' presence as civic emblems continued to pervade Salvador's streets, early to mid-nineteenth-century Candomblé leaders achieved other remarkable milestones, considering the Empire's prohibition on erecting non-Catholic holy buildings. In 1830, a few years after the first July 2 parades, three African priestesses founded the *Casa Branca de Engenho Velho*, widely recognized as Bahia's first Candomblé house (Butler 2001: 140; Cici interview Aug. 2018). Then in 1850, a high priestess from Casa Branca established another historic Candomblé, the Gantois (Castillo 2017).

10. The Christian Catholic Church exerted religious and moral influence on Bahian norms. Gayle Rubin (1984) links Christianity with sex negativity, resting "on the assumption that the genitalia are an intrinsically inferior part of the body, much lower and less holy than the mind, the 'soul,' the 'heart,' or even the upper part of the digestive system" (11). Albuquerque observes that these moral objections pivoted around values related to the socio-racial hierarchies of the times (1999: 76).

had come to associate the indigenous icons with "backwardness" and viewed them as symbols of Bahia's lack of industrial progress.[11] But despite objections to the robust dancing performed by members of popular classes at the Caboclo parades, revelers continued to express their own alternative conceptions of belonging and freedom in neighborhood celebrations of July 2. With their loose and broken qualities and lower body isolations, Candomblé's Caboclos index these layered meanings, undermine mainstream discourses of Brazilian nationalism since the inception of the state, and evoke a decolonizing aesthetic sedimented into civic commemorations of Bahian and Brazilian Independence.

Caboclos at Mãe Oba's Candomblé

As intermediaries through whom practitioner communities embody individual and collective imaginaries of political self-determination and social justice, Caboclos sing in Brazilian Portuguese and enjoy a special status in Mãe Oba's household. Spatially removed from the city center and from the more centrally located temples most implicated in the development of Candomblé's orthodox discourses and aesthetics,[12] Oba's Candomblé house sits on Travessa Augusta in São Caetano, one of Salvador's densely populated Black neighborhoods, North of the touristic areas. São Caetano borders the São Bartolomeu park, a region historically occupied by Tupinamba peoples and in which the maroon community of Urubu thrived in the nineteenth century.[13]

Though highly populated with multiple commercial centers, many residents refer to São Caetano as a "favela," inferring governmental neglect, unplanned development, and usually, a lack of security.[14] The fact that the neighborhood does not receive regular municipal services and has a reputation for criminal activity is symptomatic of its favela ranking and the lack of formal economic opportunity available to many denizens. Taxi drivers, with the exception of those from the neighborhood or adjacent precinct themselves, repeatedly refused to go all the way there during my research tenures in 2018 and 2019.

At the end of a dead-end street, the temporal-spatial zone in which Mãe Oba and her daughters conduct their ritual and domestic works holds a tenuous relationship to the systems of power that govern the distribution of resources,

---

11. Quoted from the Black journal "O Alabama" in Albuquerque 1999.

12. And from the gaze of foreigners, intellectuals, and elite Bahians, which some scholars argue has been a constitutive factor in the establishment of Candomblé's orthodox codes (i.e., Capone 2010).

13. Barbosa (2015). *Poder de Zeferina*.

14. A favela typically springs from residents' initiatives and use of accessible materials, rather than being conceived by urban planners and constructed by developers. The term favela is controversial, connoting "slum" in popular discourse, and often carrying implications of high crime and drug traffic.

including city services such as street cleaning and trash pick-up. In the morning after the annual Caboclo festival in July 2019, as I was helping sweep the premises of last night's refuse, I heard several initiates shout, "*lixo!*" (garbage!). They jumped into high gear, shoveling disposable plastic cups, yesterday's offerings, and the vestiges of the sacrificial meal quickly into heavy garbage bags. "The truck is here!" declared Barbara, a middle-aged and soft-spoken initiate, as she motioned for me to pass the dustpan. Not understanding the urgency, I asked "but when will it pass again?" "We never know!" she responded, "Whenever the sanitation workers feel like coming up." While the Candomblé compound is not geographically located uphill from a main road, Barbara uses the term "subir" or "come up" to imply the physical separation of the compound, nested deep in the neighborhood, from the regulated routes of the municipality.

The landscapes from which Caboclos hail—including Bahian backlands and Atlantic forests—are, similarly, geographically and socio-economically marginalized from the urban part of the state. These identifications bisect the practitioners' own *habitus*, a concept proposed by sociologist Pierre Bordieu (1980) to describe how power is culturally shaped in the interplay of agency and structure within a given human environment. Habitus encompasses the composite ways that social processes form individual attitudes and cognitive patterns as well as postures and movement habits (Bourdieu 1977, 1984; Wacquant 2004). While Candomblé's Africanist gods, the Orixás, inhabit celestial realms and represent moral ideals, Caboclos inhabit everyday social worlds, as well as occupations, to which practitioners can relate. Candomblé's Caboclos and their devotees share elements of the cultural and cognitive patterning that Bordieu attributes to habitus as a determinant factor in the ways that people think, feel, and act, as laborers entangled in and disadvantaged by capitalist systems of the New World.

Yet as spirit entities able to manifest in human form, Caboclos also fragment space and transcend the limitations of their social locations, embodying collective and personal freedom from exploitative conditions, and validating the pursuit of bodily pleasures such as dancing, singing, and socializing. Due to a lack of formal economic opportunities combined with race and class exclusions, practitioners in low-income neighborhoods such as Mãe Oba's often engage in a constant "hustle," laboring steadily while continuing to experience precarity in housing and employment. Caboclos' honorable work ethics and dedication to their livelihoods, in conjunction with their subjection to ongoing inequities, resonate with the quotidian experiences of many devotees while reflecting and even siphoning their desires for political and corporeal autonomy and well-deserved material recognitions. At Mãe Oba's Candomblé, and others, Caboclos are known as "donos da terra," the "lords of the land," or Brazil's original sovereigns, while their sambas speak of resilience through their distinct aesthetic virtues and narratives.

Mãe Oba toured as a dancer and then seamstress for Bahia's *Balé Folclorico* (Folkloric Ballet), and several of her initiates dance professionally and teach for the company. When I first met Mãe Oba, I was familiar with several dancers and choreographers who frequented her terreiro, from my training in Salvador's

Figure 6 Caboclo Sete Flexas embodied by Mãe Oba. Photograph by Orleans Junior.

Afro-Bahian dance and percussion classes. I thus entered the temple community as a race and language outsider but a dance insider. Through participating in samba at Mãe Oba's festas, over time, some of the social boundaries between myself and other women devotees became porous enough for me to be invited into their complex intimacies forged by ritual kinship. Certainly, Mãe Oba and initiates at her house are well versed in Orixá choreographies and rhythms, and in the vernacular differences between Orixá movements adapted for the stage and the more roots versions typically performed in ceremony. However, the sambas at Mãe Oba's house, full of inflections, and orated through call-and-response verses, articulate with the popular expressive styles of the favela and the lack of spatial and conceptual distance between audience and participants in street samba cyphers and in the temple space (interview Escola de dança, FUNCEB, 2018).

The Decolonizing Aesthetics of Candomblé's Caboclo Embodiments

In a discussion about Caboclo aesthetics, one practitioner, Eduardo Fonseca, commented that samba engages the "fragmented daily experience of living on the margins, in the favela" (interview, June 25, 2018). Via its Afro-Bahian origins and associations with the favela, samba is both racialized and coded as working class. Yet in national discourses, the racial and class complexities indexed by samba's interlacing with African identity are subsumed by mythologizations of Brazil's history of miscegenation as a benign blending of African and European cultures leading to a utopic racial democracy.[15] When discussing the dance, Eduardo links the qualities of loose and broken to the lack of separation between the space of the dance and quotidian life in the urban favelas of Rio and Bahia, where samba emerged and continues to be innovated upon, and that are populated by socio-economically underprivileged, mostly Afro-descendent, Brazilians.[16] In this sense, samba also epitomizes the dialogue between personal agency and social structure that defines habitus, as a set of dispositions that shape current practices and condition our sense of place (Bordieu 1977). The Caboclos' loose and broken ways of moving, embodied in an accented lunge and recovery, or the polycentric shake of the shoulders on top of the hips, effectively fragment the space of the body and the space between performers, while creating intimacy in the form of a close and playful confrontation.

Distinguished from the samba of Rio's annual Carnaval, where dancers broadcast their movements to audiences on raised platforms along the sides of a massive stadium, Caboclo sambas propose a participatory mode in 360-degree spatiality, playing with the fragmentation of the body in the closed space of the cypher, where distance is not possible. Caboclos dance their sambas in tight spaces, rubbing up against drummers and other festa-goers. Both Rio's samba, called *samba no pé* or samba in the feet because of its quick footwork, and the Caboclo sambas are based on the triple-step foot shuffle of the *samba de roda* practiced by African descendents on Bahia's colonial plantations. While the sambas of Rio's Carnaval depart from the round format, with dancers on elevated and televised stages, samba de roda and the Caboclos' sambas share a circular structure in which performers rotate in and out of the center, alternately becoming viewers and dancers. Performer and audience roles interchange in overlapping segments of time.

15. Freyre 1939; see also Vianna 2000 and Bishop-Sanchez 2015.
16. Structured discussion at UFBA, May 28, 2018.

Figure 7 A cowboy Caboclo steps to the side of the circle to become a spectator at Ilê Omin Guiam, Itaparica Island, Caboclo festival, August 2018. Still from author's video.

This dynamic, improvised exchange precludes the possibility of establishing a fixed gaze and makes passive consumption of the samba dancer's performance impossible, especially since a viewer is likely to be drawn into the circle. Though Caboclos' dancing and Rio's Carnaval sambas both utilize fast, syncopated footwork and body part isolations, the commercial success of Rio's Carnaval banks on mediatized images of mixed-race, female samba dancers in revealing, g-string costumes and feathered headdresses resonate with hegemonic constructions of Black Brazilian women's sexual availability.[17] As anthropologist Natasha Pravaz notes, Rio samba dancers' bodies "are on display for visual consumption and have become multifocal symbols eliciting associations that resonate both with colonial morality and with *mestiçagem*, the narrative of racial and cultural mixing as a cornerstone of nationhood" (2012: 113).[18] In the samba circle of Candomblé

17. While some scholars have analyzed the *mulata* figure in Brazilian and Cuban dance (i.e., Bianco Borelli) and in representations of Indigenous identity in Carnaval (i.e., Roach), the feathered headdress associated with Rio samba aesthetics, as well as various Caribbean Carnaval traditions, is a particularly enduring and performative object linking representations of Indigenous identity and the Caboclo to sexualized discourses of Brazilian nationhood.

18. Pravaz explores how Rio's "mulatas" (mixed-race samba dancers) must "manipulate the objectifying gaze of Brazilians and foreigners" while they "attempt to portray their dance skills as culturally 'authentic' in the search for legitimacy and racial pride" (2012: 114). Rosa (2015) charges Brazil's foremost TV station, Globo, with depicting samba dancing mulatas as exoticized objects, in ways that have long been typical of disseminated imagery about Brazil.

ceremony, Caboclos riff on, twist, and trouble samba's legacies of exoticization, destabilizing these processes of objectification through tactics such as switching viewer/performer roles, exaggerated interest in women's dancing bodies—through facial expression and body position—and gender-fluid embodiments that I will explore shortly.

Pursuing this aesthetic comparison a little longer, Rio's samba performers typically use high-heeled sandals and extend their elbows to emphasize long lines that frame the body even as the feet and hips oscillate at incredible speed. In Caboclo sambas, dancers maintain grounded, flexed hips, knees, and elbows in order to quickly change direction, or to react to a musician or another dancer, while staying connected to the earthen floor beneath their feet. In contrast, partly because of the restrictive heavy headdress and sequined bikini typically used for costuming, samba no pé dancers typically employ upright presentational postures.

Caboclos fragment and break these lines as they break with dominant standards of behavior and appearance conditioned through colonial morality and the objectifying representational schemas that mark Rio's Carnaval. Relative to the vernacular styles of Rio samba, and samba de roda, where torso articulations are generally more understated, Caboclo sambas feature accented falls and breaks that take dancers off their vertical axes. These breaks infuse performances with a sense of discontinuity and surprise in relation to the dance action, and allow improvisors to experiment widely with personal style, phrasing, and tone.

In a recent class, percussion and dance teacher Zé Ricardo, who also frequents Mãe Oba's Candomblé house, announced cheekily to a group of professionally trained dancers that: "Caboclos have no aesthetic." Then, lengthening his arms and legs in reference to the Rio samba style and to the ballet training he has in common with the majority of the present students, he clarified: "What I mean is, they don't have *this* aesthetic" (Samba Congress, Toronto, June 2019). Ricardo's point was well understood by dancers trained to elongate their wrists, arms, and legs to create "classical" lines. Caboclo practices *do* operate in accordance with guiding principles that overarch their costuming, oral traditions, and movements, but these codes differ from the aesthetics of the proscenium theatrical stage. The divergence from Western concert dance aesthetics that Ricardo refers to is part of the Caboclos' unique standards of beauty and elegance that privilege elements of surprise, spontaneity, provocation, and even acts of refusal that counterpoint social and ceremonial norms.

For example, whereas in Orixá ceremony the rhythms and liturgies proceed in specified order and are initiated by a designated caller, in a Caboclo festa a samba verse can be initiated by an entity, participant, or musician. Caboclos frequently, sometimes obstinately, demand that musicians stop, start, or change their playing, and, at the end of a long night, they may refuse to leave—and release the drummers and ritual leaders—until the commitments of the night have been fulfilled to their satisfaction. Relative to the strict systems of Orixá initiation and ceremony, Caboclo festas are characterized by these permeable boundaries of participation. At a festa I attended in October 2018, Caboclo guardians of the host terreiro, already embodied by their daughters and sons of the saint, made a point of dancing in close proximity to visitors, in order to entice new and perhaps unknown entities to the festivities. At the same ceremony, one particular cowboy Caboclo roused the crowd regularly whenever the energy dropped, pulling observers into the circle over and over again.

Caboclos' penchant for improvisation reflects what anthropologist Brian Brazeal deems their "pragmatic efficacy," which depends on the dialogical call and response between ritual participants rather than on a "conceptual or theological system of beliefs." Focusing his research on Caboclo music, Brazeal proposes that, since knowledge about the Caboclo pantheon is contained in the repertoire of songs they sing, rather than in an elaborate mythology as it is for the Orixá pantheon, ceremonies held in honor of the Caboclos are contexts in which hierarchies can be challenged and reasserted (2003: 642). Looking particularly at how Caboclos disembody hierarchies embedded in colonial arrangements, the next section focuses on how a samba performed by a cowboy Caboclo disrupts racial and sexual power dynamics linked to the historical space of the plantation.

Boiadeiro's "Rough" Samba

The samba songs and dances I observed and participated in over the course of my fieldwork exemplify Caboclos' resilient aesthetic and existential condition, in which rupture and fragmentation operate as structuring principles of experience. One song in particular foregrounds the linkage between practitioners' social conditions, Caboclos' spatial and economic marginalization, and samba's loose, broken, and rebounding corporealities. Here, the Caboclo cowboy or Boiadeiro sings of how the Master's daughter beckoned him to attend to her inside of the Big house.

> The daughter of the big house sent her servant for me X2
> I sent him to tell her, I am minding your cattle
> Olo Boiadeiro, he likes a rough samba X2
> A menina do sobrado, mandou me chamar por seu criado X2
> Eu mandei dizer a ela, estou vaquejando o seu gado
> Olo Boiadeiro, ele gosta do samba rasgado X2.[19]

In this stanza the samba "rasgado," loosely translated as "rough," stands in counterpoint to a visit to the Master house. Boiadeiro states his wish to stay amidst the cattle on the ranch rather than become involved in the affairs of the implicitly white daughter of the plantation owner. The cowboy, rejecting the class hierarchies that would obligate him to obey the commands from the daughter of the big house, prefers to stay out in the fields with his cows and dance a "samba

---

19. Translations from Brazilian Portuguese to English by the author in consulation with Cici de Oxalá.

rasgado." By calling for a samba rasgado, Boiadeiro implores the musicians at the festa to play more intensely and quickly for him.

A colloquialism when used in this sense, "rasgado" can infer rough or robust qualities; a fast and "cut" or staccato samba rhythm on which to dance. Cristiam, a medium from a neighboring Candomblé to Mãe Oba's, adds the meanings "non-stop, fluent or fluid, fast and continuous" (Oct. 23, 2019). Another interlocutor, Sandro, defines "rasgado" as pertaining exclusively to the province of Boiadeiro's samba, signifying a style that is "beautiful, well played, *well* danced"[20] (October 24, 2019). This positive aesthetic valuation concords with Africanist aesthetic terms that have been noted by art and dance historians, including the skillful correlation of choreography and music, the "sinuous" or serpentine movement of the spine (Rosa 2015), and the intensity of juxtaposition between fast and slower-paced rhythms and between the dancer's seemingly effortless "coolness" (Thompson 1984) and the highly proficient execution of complex footwork.

The lyrics of Boiadeiro's verse collapse the space of the ranch with the ceremonial wheel while aurally and corporeally linking the samba's rough loose, broken movements and call-and-response dialogue with the marginal outback that he inhabits, outside the control of the Master's daughter and the Master himself, an exemplar of bourgeois colonial masculinity. When he comes riding into the sanctuary, Boiadeiro comes mounted on his horse with all the rebellious fervor implied in the song, from one space distally related to the nexus of socio-economic order (represented by the big house), the outlying fields of the ranch, to another, São Caetano and the Mãe Oba's Candomblé compound or *terreiro*.

I want to draw attention to the analogous relation between the Boiadeiro's position on the ranch in the samba lyric and the terreiro populace's positioning in a dense but peripheral urban nucleus. The field, beyond the view and reach of the plantation owner, though officially within the domain of the property, could proffer a parallel to the Candomblé house as a historic and contemporaneous space of Afro-Bahian refuge, only slightly insulated from Brazil's postcolonial politics and the threat of police violence.[21] The field, like the temple, constitutes a

---

20. "bonito, bem tocado, *bem* dançado." Other interpretations of "rasgado" include: "Rasgado is fast, but also truncated" (Silva, interview, 2019). "Rasgado in some contexts can mean straightforward or blunt. I believe that samba rasgado has the context of pure samba, genuine samba, root samba. The cabrocha [mulata, country girl] brings rustic samba, without ornaments, from the hill to the city." (D'Angelis, personal communication 2019). "It has many meanings but overall, it is a samba that's non-stop. Fluent, fast, intense and continuous" (Fonseca, interview, 2019).

21. Journalist Marques Travae reports that police in Bahia "kill more than one person per day," a rate higher than Rio and São Paulo (as well as US cities). Though statistical figures are difficult to verify due to the ways that police homicides are classified (see Smith 2016), *Black Brazil Today* lists that, of 706 police killings of youth aged 15–29 in 2004, 699 (99 percent) were Black and seven were white (September 21, 20121). One of Mãe Oba's grandsons was killed by police during a 2020 raid in São Caetano.

privileged but still risky site of decolonial praxis. Standing there, Boiadeiro enjoys semi-autonomy from the domicile and its threat of unwanted inter-racial sex suggested by the Master's daughter; at the same time, as a worker his livelihood depends on the ability to get along in the normative labor laws of the plantation system. Similarly, Mãe Oba's constituents generally occupy a place that is at once outside of the metropole, in terms of access to services, yet firmly situated inside of it geographically; they depend on the city for basic needs like security, electricity, and transportation, to name a few. But the ceremonial universe of the temple also reformulates the established social structure, through ritual kinships and the counter-discourses produced in performance.

While the unpredictability of resource access has structuring effects on the lives of ritual practitioners today, the mestiço cowboy enacted in the samba is able to undermine the power structure by choosing to remain in the field, where he is master of his own body and movements, rather than submit to the hierarchical social order of the big house. The cowboy here is situated in the historical context of the plantation system of the past. His implication within the New World economy and his subaltern location at the intersection of colonial race and class systems make his identity and livelihood relatable to devotees, while his loose and beautiful samba embodies the idealized qualities that free him from the constraints that the plantation power structure of the past seeks to impose on his body, spirit, and psyche.

The samba rasgado—cut, beautiful, and full of breaks—disputes the sexual-political subservience ascribed to the cowboy by the Master's daughter (who as the bearer of racialized, patriarcho-colonial authority also represents a seat of power in the system of white domination) while re-framing the field as a site for the assertion of radical self-possession.[22] The cowboy's samba rasgado establishes a terrain of corporeal autonomy in the field, in contrast to the call of the Master's daughter toward the homestead where his Afro-indigenous body could likely be objectified through the legal relations of settler colonialism. In the above example, a space of defiant contestation opens up in the cowboy's dancing, in which the grip of the Master house and its power geometries on Boiadeiro's person are effectively loosened.

When I returned to Bahia in the following year, I witnessed another remarkable example of how Caboclo practices trouble moral-sexual and erotic hierarchies steeped in colonial value systems. Because by this point in my research I had completed several cursory rites of passage at Mãe Oba's Candomblé, my ritual obligations included dancing in the opening circle. In turn, I was able to perceive

---

22. In this passage, white patriarchy is embodied by the master's daughter and not the master himself. This narrative twist could point to ways that racial power dynamics supersede gender hierarchies so that, marked by whiteness and owning class status, the daughter's efforts to subjugate the cowboy to her will operate as attempts to extend the reach of the plantation house's social hierarchies to the field.

Figure 8 A Boiadeiro dancing before the drummers at Ilê Omin Guiam, Itaparica Island, Caboclo festival, August 2018. Still from author's video.

the ceremony from within the center of the sanctuary, close to and inside of the intimate sambas that transpired near the end of the evening. One of these duos involved the senior priestess, Mãe Oba, and a younger initiate circling with his Boiadeiro. The next section examines their provocative duet, showing how the dance opens a space that allows practitioners to refigure hetero-patriarchal norms around giving and receiving pleasure, in a ceremonial context that normalizes diverse forms of material and kinetic gift exchange.

Dancing in the "Outer Limits": Sete and Boiadeiro's Intimate Duet

Sete Flexas (Seven Arrows) is the guardian Caboclo of Mãe Oba's house. He is a hyper-masculine, Indigenous-identified entity, depicted as a beer-drinking bull on the poster taped to the temple's front door. Sete's arrival and enjoyment are a key goal of Mãe Oba's annual Caboclo festa. Sharing agency with Mãe Oba when he embodies her and dances with another Caboclo at the ceremony held in his honor, their performance transgresses dominant moral and religious codes to valorize women's illegitimized pleasures and desires, and affirm the capacity of male-bodied, masculinized subjects to satisfy those desires.

After the Caboclos have arrived and then dressed, they re-enter the sanctuary as the percussionists begin to play with bare hands slapping the skins of their well-fed goat-skin drums. Taína, one of Oba's granddaughters, has incarnated her Boiadeiro. She appears as a macho man in a woman's body, a bit hunched over, with clunky samba steps that narrate the Caboclo riding in on his horse, and eyes that dwell on the ladies' behinds. In this trans-embodiment typical of Caboclo ceremony, Taína's Boiadeiro dances with his knees apart in the samba style associated with masculine performance. In Bahian Candomblé, women-identified mediums circling with male divinities are germane to orthodox, Africanist Orixá practices as well as rituals linked to the transgressive lineages of Brazilian Exus and Caboclos. However, the Caboclos are unique in their extreme bending of gender expectations and their use of satire that brings the constructedness of gender and sex categories into relief. Reflecting Candomblé diction, I refer to female mediums embodying male entities using the pronoun "he." But, importantly, the active status of mediumship makes the assignment of binary gender impossible and renders the bodies involved resistant to gender categorization.

The Boiadero's attention moves to a middle-aged woman with the folds of her colorful skirt tucked into the waist to avoid tripping up her flying feet. Responding to the Caboclo's encouragement, she willingly turns around to show him the effect of her shuffling footwork on her swinging hips. Another medium, Barbara, has also become embodied by her Boiadeiro. He wears a brimmed leather cap, wide-legged brown pants, and a decorated vest. This Caboclo keeps his legs in a wide straddle, digging alternate heels into the earth as his body tips sideways to counterbalance the low-slung weight shifts. The Caboclos come in and out of the sanctuary and the internal rooms of the temple, getting drinks and smokes which their caretakers light for them. One of Mãe Oba's daughters, Zeulma, becomes embodied by a Caboclo *de pena*, or "feathered" Caboclo, the Sultan of the Forests. He dons an impressive headdress of white feathers that slings back when he lunges forward. He turns around, pointing a foot or shoulder toward another dancer as an invitation for the next performer to come into the circle.

Manifested in the body of Mãe Oba, Sete Flexas appears on the periphery of the circle. The guests kneel to the floor in respect of his entrance. Tiago, a younger, muscular medium in his early twenties and circling with his agile Boiadeiro, inches forward on his knees until his torso approaches Sete Flexa's groin. Sete's arrival signifies a pivotal moment of the ceremony and suggests the fulfillment and continuation of his contract with the congregation. Encouraged by Sete's appearance and the duo's lively display, the other Caboclos sing loudly and the drumming accelerates. The young initiate's face rests few inches away from Sete Flexa's moving pelvis. Sete opens and bends his legs as he inches forward in space, urging the cowboy Caboclo into a deep limbo backwards until his neck reaches an angle almost parallel to the sanctuary floor, while his face and Sete Flexas's pelvis stay in close proximity. Sete's facial expression admits pleasure bordering on whimsy.

While their physical demeanors suggest oral sexual activity, the feeling that charges their exchange is one of playful desire, such that the intimacy shared by the entities and by the executive bodies of their hosts supports a politics of pleasure that, following feminist theorist Joan Morgan, links sexual expression and erotic agency to liberatory Black feminist imperative (2015). Sete Flexas, encircled with Mãe Oba, occupies an empowered position in both the social structure of the temple and in the physical dynamics of the dance. At the same time, their performance makes use of erotic language to confirm the complementary alliances of the two gods—Sete Flexas and Tiago's Boiadeiro—while also situating Sete Flexas, whose embodied presence is shared with and co-produced by his host, the high priestess, as the recipient of sexual pleasure that clearly confirms both his powerful ranking as the governing regent of the Candomblé house and the authority of the high priestess in her right to receive and exchange pleasure.

This performance locates Mãe Oba, embodied by Sete Flexas, in an active position, while Tiago's Boiadeiro takes on the relatively submissive posture of "giving," when viewed through the lens of Brazilian sexual idioms (see Browning 1995; Green 1999). The duet between Sete Flexas (in the body of a senior female) and Boiadeiro (in the body of a young male) thus conjoins the display of masculine sexual assertiveness with a markedly anti-patriarchal expression of female sexual pleasure. Furthermore, with Mãe Oba and her Caboclo in the active and dominant position, the duet configures the matriarch's erotic subjectivity as itself propitious of the terreiro's social reproduction, a "considered source of power and information" to embrace, in the words of Audré Lorde (1978, 88). Lorde's framework of "the erotic as the nurturer and nursemaid of all of our deepest knowledge" (89) is especially illuminating here, since, in Candomblé, the *mãe de santo* or priestess constitutes the ultimate catalyst for the movement and multiplication of *axé*, metaphysical muscle, or ritual efficaciousness.

Although the two human persons in question, Mãe Oba and Tiago, present as female and male-sexed, respectively, the act of being embodied by entities whose gender and sex identities may or may not differ from those of the mediums marks their encounters as gender-fluid and impervious to ascriptions of binary homo- or hetero-sexuality, just as they resist binary understandings of gender. When read according to the bodies involved in the duo and the Brazilian categories of active and passive sexual behavior, however, the performance inverts the normative gender roles of active masculinized figure and passive female, where, unlike Western understandings of sexual exchange, "giving" in Brazilian parlance corresponds to the passive position while receiving or "eating" is ascribed to the active position. Even if Sete Flexas and Boiadeiro, circling with Mãe Oba and Tiago, appear as a heterosexual couple, their duo is charged with homo-social tones that are evident to ceremonial participants versed in Candomblé's relational constructions of the body.

These multivalent sexual registers of Sete and Boiadeiro's intimate performance transgress the boundaries of erotic behavior condoned by bourgeois Brazilian sex ideologies in the nineteenth and twentieth centuries. Brazilian elites in the late 1800s were highly influenced by European ideological currents including medical models having to do with fixed, rather than contextual, divisions of heterosexual and homosexual preference, fears of male transvestism, and paternalistic concern with women's occupational activities outside of the domestic household (Green 1999; Cowan 2016). This period proved ripe for the consolidation of socio-erotic hierarchies similar to sexual taxonomies based on Victorian morality and Christian attitudes toward sex that coalesced in the United States.

The foundations of Victorian-Christian sex taboos, which continue to inform public policy and popular opinion today, are addressed by feminist anthropologist Gayle Rubin (1984). Rubin outlines what she terms the "charmed circle" of sex acts preserved through legislation, policing, medical practice, and moral discourse, for purposes including control over women's reproductive rights and the criminalization of prostitution as a social threat. Rubin details how various sexual acts are deemed "good, normal, natural and blessed," namely, banal heterosexual procreative encounters between same-age married partners at home. On the other hand, the charmed circle consigns nonheterosexual, public, nonmonogamous erotic acts involving consenting inter-generational partners or more than two people to the "outer limits" of acceptability. These acts are "'bad,' 'abnormal' or 'unnatural'" and, often, politically reprehensible (14).[23]

While Rubin deals with explicitly sexual activities, I want to be clear that I am addressing erotics in the broad sense; the performances described here do not involve any actual physical contact. It is precisely the absence of physical contact that makes Caboclos' gestures resonate dually as ironic critiques of sex norms based on Christian moral codes hierarchies and as affirmations of pleasure as a productive mode and valuable resource.[24] These moral ideologies also embed class and race hegemonies by virtue of privileging state-sanctioned marriages rejected by many women of Candomblé, and align with seigniorial models of virginal or matrimonial womanhood from Brazil's post-abolition Republican era (Landes 1947; Filho 2019).

In addition to the "political reprehensibility" of the duo's samba in terms of their visibility in the public ceremonial sphere, age difference, nonmonogamous relationship of ritual kinship (which elides recognition by the state) and potential homosocial and pan-sexual connotations, Sete and Boiadeiro's dance breaks with normative social and kinetic scripts of space and bodily proximity. During the invocation circle, devotees maintain fairly vertical body composure, leaning to one side and another while slightly bent at the hips but keeping an overall sense

23. Rubin's framework is influenced by Foucault (1978), who broadly explores how patterns of sexual desire and behavior are socially engineered, and how sexual moralities are both culturally relative and socially determined.

24. Rubin's rubric proves useful for understanding the socio-erotic hierarchies that Caboclos' break down and reformulate to emphasize the giving and receiving of pleasures that fall beyond the limits of domestic, "vanilla," heterosexual acts. Not only does the erotic hierarchy justify sexual oppression, the charmed circle, established in relation to Christian sex negativity, criminalizes subjects whose sexual practices misalign with the institution of civil marriage regulated by the state (Rubin 1984: 11).

of distance from the sanctuary floor. After embodying their daughters and sons and singing their songs of arrival, the Caboclos begin to surge forward, stoop down, leap up, and arch backward to near ninety-degree angles. These gestures dramatically shift the relationship of dancers to the earth, which becomes elastic as they move in and out of vertical stances. In the samba between Sete and the young Boiadeiro, the cowboy kneels on the concrete floor before Sete Flexas, breaking with patterns of upright verticality and using his torso and facial expression to draw attention to the lower body of the incorporated priestess. Boiadeiro's low posture—as he kneels on the ground with his face just below the groin belonging to Mãe Oba's body—violates standards of respectability that pervade even today's codes of permissible conduct on dedicated dance club floors in Brazil.[25]

Sete Flexas and Boiadeiro, dancing their provocative duo, engage what is normatively perceived as "the profane" inside the sanctuary space; Sete accentuates the lower extremities as he gets down, while Boiadeiro's bodily posture draws even more attention to Sete Flexa's pelvis and hip rotations.[26] Yet, while the Caboclos' dancing seems transgressive according to social norms of comportment and the aristocratic standards of the Orixá, their movements actually nest within a vast range of acceptable styles for Caboclo ceremony. The duet between Sete Flexas and Boiadeiro, furthermore, creates an aura around the temple's matriarch (in collaboration with the command of her Caboclo, Sete Flexas), which fiercely contrasts the image of the asexual, sweet, giving, Black Mother that James Matory (2005) ties to nationalist mythologies of Candomblé's female leaders.

The subversive potential represented by Candomblé's spaces of Black cultural empowerment and citizenship has been conceptually pacified, according to Matory, by personifications of senior female priestesses as "self-sacrificial, self-effacing, long-suffering, generous, constantly available" and "equally maternal to blacks and whites" (202). This vocabulary of reference applied by journalists

25. Bakhtin (1984) is relevant here. The aesthetics of grotesque realism (18) that he attributes to medieval cultures of folk humor develop around a "material body principle" that engages the continual growth and renewal of the people. Caboclos' sambas evince this material body principle by emphasizing images of fertility, sexual vitality, and attraction in their movements, facial expressions of interest, and spoken commentaries. Differentiating his subject from bourgeois identifications, Bakhtin's argument that leading images of fertility and abundance belong to the "collective ancestral body" and not the biological individual or private ego of the "economic man" (19) resonates with the ritual contexts of interrelation, where individual persons share their bodies and subjectivities with spirit entities whose energy refracts and builds upon the pretext of collective participation.

26. In her discussion of Candomblé's Caboclo, Barbara Browning notes that although "the term *samba* to designate the caboclo spirit's dance seems to be a way of blurring the distinction between the divine and the profane," the Caboclo himself is "intent on breaking down barriers, releasing strictures such as those between the sacred and the secular" (1995: 26).

to various Candomblé matriarchs of the last 100 years exemplifies the "nostalgic, infantile, and narcissistic dreams of the privileged class in a postslavery society," (200). For Matory, these ideations of Candomblé's "Black Mothers" are rooted in their apparent similarity to the beloved, plump, and wise Mammy-like nursemaid character from Brazilian literary representations of the colonial household.[27]

Framed by the young Boiadeiro's embodied by Tiago, and by the rest of the congregation's enjoyment of the scene, the Black Mother of the house, Mãe Oba, appears far from self-effacing or docile. As the recipient of pleasure and effigy of delight, her in-the-flesh presence fragments colonialist fantasies of a sexually inactive and politically pacified Afro-Bahian womanhood. Rather, Mãe Oba figures clearly as the active recipient and consumer of ecstasy that will be reproduced to ensure the beneficial reproduction of axé in the community. The pleasures of the terreiro's matriarch are sedimented into a religious and cosmo-aesthetic imperative allied to the fulfillment of the congregation's ritual contract with their primary Caboclo protector. Dancing loose and broken sambas, senior and novice initiates of Candomblé's Caboclos at Mãe Oba's house affirm a feminist politics that corrodes the colonial pairing of black bodies with labour exploitation and the denial of pleasure and locates women's erotic knowledges at the nexus of spiritual empowerment.

Bibliography

Albuquerque, Wlamyra. "Civismo popular, algazarra nas ruas: comemorações da independência nacional na Bahia" ("Popular Civic Spirit, Uproar in the Streets: Celebrations of National Independence in Bahia." *IdeAs. Idées d'Amériques* 20 (2022). https://doi.org/10.4000/ideas.14170.

Bakhtin, Mikhael. *Rabelais and His World*. Bloomington: Indiana University Press, 1984.

Banerji, Anurima. *Dancing Odissi: Paratopic Performances of Gender and State*. Calcutta: Seagull Books, 2019, 31–2.

Barbosa, Silvia Maria Silva. *Poder de Zeferina No Quilombo Do Urubu: Uma reconstrução histórica politico-social*. London: Novas Edições Acadêmicas, 2015.

Barbosa, Terezinha (Mãe Oba). Interviews with the author. May 2018, September 24, 2018, July 10, 2019, December 9, 2019, June 1, 2020, and August 25, 2020. Salvador, Bahia, Brazil.

Bastide, Roger. *The African Religions of Brazil: Toward a Sociology of the Interpenetration of Civilizations*. Baltimore and London: Johns Hopkins Press, 1960.

Bishop-Sanchez, Katherine, Medeiros Albuquerque, and Severino João, eds. *Performing Brazil: Essays on Culture, Identity and the Performing Arts*. Madison, WI: University of Wisconsin Press, 2015.

27. Northeastern Regionalist writer Gilberto Freyre's Masters and the Slaves (1934) is the seminal text for the foundational narrative of *mestiçagem* (miscegenation) as the force behind the nation's cultural singularity at the junction of European, African, and Native civilization.

Bourdeiu, Pierre. *Outline of a Theory of Practice*. Cambridge: Cambridge University Press, 1977.

Bourdeiu, Pierre. *Distinction: A Social Critique of the Judgment of Taste*. London: Routledge & Kegan Paul, 1984.

Brazeal, Brian. "The Music of the Bahian Caboclos." *Anthropological Quarterly* 76, no. 4 (2003): 642.

Browning, Barbara. *Samba: Resistance in Motion*. Bloomington: Indiana University Press, 1995.

Butler, Kim. "Africa in the Reinvention of Nineteenth Century Afro-Bahian Identity, Slavery & Abolition." *A Journal of Slave and Post-Slave Studies* 22, no. 1 (2001): 135–54.

Capoeira, Nestor. *Capoeira: Roots of the Dance-Fight-Game*. Berkeley, CA: North Atlantic Books, 2002.

Capone, Stefania. *Searching for Africa in Brazil: Power and Tradition in Candomblé*. Durham: Duke University Press, 2010.

Castillo, Lisa Earl. "Entre memória, mito e história: viajantes transatlânticos da Casa Branca." In *Escravidão e suas sombras*, org. by João José REIS and Elciene Azevedo, 65–110. Salvador: UFBA, 2012.

Castillo, Lisa Earl. "Terreiro do Gantois: Redes Socias e Etnografia Histórica no Século XIX." *Rev. Hist.* (São Paulo) n. 176 (2017): a05616.

Cowan, Benjamin. *Securing Sex: Morality and Repression in the Making of Cold War Brazil*. Chapel Hill: University of North Carolina Press, 2016.

D'Angelis, André. Personal Communication. May 10, 2019. Toronto, Canada.

Dixon-Gottschild, Brenda. *Digging the Africanist Presence in American Performance: Dance and Other Contexts*. Westport, CT: Greenwood Press, 1996.

Filho, Alberto Ferreira. "Desafricanizar as ruas: elites letradas, mulheres pobres e cultura popular em Salvador (1890–1937)." *Afro-Ásia* no. 21–2 (1999 [1998]): 239–56. https://periodicos.ufba.br/index.php/afroasia/issue/view/1457.

Fonseca, Cristiam. Interview. April 15, 2018. Salvador, Bahia, Brazil.

Fonseca, Cristiam. Personal Communication. *Web Correspondence*. May 29, 2019.

Foster, Susan Leigh. "Choreographies of Gender" *Signs* (Autumn, 1998), 1–33.

Foster, Susan Leigh. "Choreographies of Protest." *Theatre Journal* 55 no. 3 (2003): 395–412.

Foucault, Michel. *History of Sexuality*. New York: Pantheon Books, 1978.

Freyre, Gilberto. *The Masters and the Slaves*. Rio de Janeiro: Maia. & Schmidt, Ltd., 1934.

Glynn, George A. "Foreign Constitutions : Comprising the Constitution of Argentine, Belgium, Brazil (empire and republic), Columbia, Ecuador, France, Germany, Honduras, Japan, Mexico, Prussia, Switzerland and Venezuela Prepared in Prusuance of Chapter 8, of Laws of 1893, and Chapter 228 of Laws of 1894." *The Convention Manual of the Sixth New York State Constitutional Convention*, 55–106. Albany: Argus Co., 1984.

Green, James. *Beyond Carnival: Male Homosexuality in Twentieth Century Brazil*. Chicago: University of Chicago Press, 1999.

Harding, Rachel E. *A Refuge in Thunder: Candomblé and Alternative Spaces of Blackness*. Bloomington and Indianapolis: Indiana University Press, 2000.

Landes, Ruth. *City of Women*. New York: The Macmillan Co., 1947.

Lior, Mika Lillit. *Circling with/in The Saint: Bahian Candomblé's Feminist Poiesis and Dark Horse Kinetics*. University of California, Los Angeles, 2021. https://escholarship.org/uc/item/6jh2f06m.

Lior, Mika Lillit. Notes. Caboclo festa, Ilê Axé Oba Ina, Salvador, Brazil. August 20, 2019.

Lorde, Audre. *Uses of the Erotic: the Erotic as Power*. Trumansburg, NY: Out & Out Books, 1978.

Matory, James Lorand. *Black Atlantic Religion: Tradition, Transnationalism, and Matriarchy in the Afro-Brazilian Candomblé*. Princeton: Princeton University Press, 2005.

Morgan, Joan. "Why We Get Off: Moving towards a Black Feminist Politics of Pleasure." *The Black Scholar* 4, no. 36 (2015): 36–46.

Parés, Luis Nicolau. *The Formation of Candomblé: Vodun History and Ritual in Brazil.* Translated by Richard Vernon and L. N. Parés. Chapel Hill: University of North Carolina Press, 2013 [2006].

Prandi, Reginaldo. *Encantaria brasileira: O livro dos mestres, caboclos e encantados* (Portuguese Edition). Rio de Janeiro: Pallas, 2001.

Pravaz, Natasha. "Performing Mulata-Ness: The Politics of Cultural Authenticity and Sexuality among Carioca Samba Dancers." *Latin American Perspectives* 39, no. 2 (2012): 113–33.

Rabelo, Miriam. *Enredos, Feituras e Modos de Cuidado: Dimensões da vida e da convivência no Candomblé*. Salvador: EDUFBA, 2014.

Rabelo, Miriam, and Ricardo Aragão. "Caboclos e Orixás no Terreiro: modos de conexão e possibilidades de simbiose." *Religião & Sociedade* 38 (2018): 84–109.

Reis, José. "Candomblé in Nineteenth-Century Bahia: Priests, Followers, Clients." *Slavery & Abolition* 22, no. 1 (2001): 91–115.

Ribeiro, Alexandre. 2008. "The Transatlantic Slave Trade to Bahia, 1582–1851." In *Extending the Frontiers,* edited by David Eltis and David Richardson. Yale Scholarship Online, October 2008.

Rosa, Cristina. *Swing Nation: Brazilian Bodies and Their Choreographies of Identification.* London: Palgrave MacMillan, 2015.

Rubin, Gayle. "Thinking Sex: Notes for a Radical Theory of the Politics of Sexuality." In *The Lesbian and Gay Studies Reader,* edited by Henry Abelove, Michele Aina Barale and David M. Halperin, 3–42. New York: Routledge, 1993.

Schwartz, Stuart, ed. "Preface" In *Early Brazil: A Documentary Collection to 1700s,* ix–xviii. Cambridge: Cambridge University Press, 2009.

Smith, Christen A. *Afro-Paradise: Blackness, Violence, and Performance in Brazil*. Urbana, IL and Springfield: University of Illinois Press, 2016.

Souza E Silva, Nancy de (Cici, Dona). Interviews. May 7, 2018, August 19, 2018, September 21, 2018, November 2, 2018, and August 4, 2019. Salvador, Bahia, Brazil.

Sterling, Cheryl. "Women-Space, Power, and the Sacred in the Afro-Brazilian Culture." *The Global South* 4, no. 1, Special Issue: Latin America in a Global Age (Spring, 2010): 71–93.

Strongman, Roberto. *Queering Black Atlantic Religions: Transcorporeality in Candomblé, Santería, and Vodou*. Durham: Duke University Press, 2019.

Teles Dos Santos, Jocélio. "La divinité 'caboclo' dans le candomblé de Bahia." *Cahiers d'Études Africaines* 32, no. 125 (1992): 83–107.

Teles Dos Santos, Jocélio. *O dono da terra: O caboclo nos candomblés da Bahia (Portuguese Edition).* Salvador: Sarah Letras, 1995.

Teles Dos Santos, Jocélio (Coord.). *Mapeamento dos Terreiros de Salvador*. Salvador: Centro de Estudos Afros-Orientais, 2006.

Thompson, Robert Farris. *Flash of the Spirit: African and Afro-American Art and Philosophy*. New York: Random House, 1984.

Travae, Marques. "Police in Northeastern State of Bahia Kill More than One Person Per Day" in Black Brazil Today. September 21, 2012. Web.

Verger, Pierre. *Flux et reflux de la traite des nègres entre le golfe de Bénin et Bahia de Todos os Santos du dix-septième au dix-neuvième siècle*. Paris: Mouton & Co et E.P.H.E., 1976.

Vianna, Hermano. *The Mystery of Samba*: *Popular Music & National Identity in Brazil.*
	Chapel Hill: University of North Carolina Press, 1999.
Zé, Ricardo. Dance Class Lecture. Toronto Samba Congress. June 30, 2019.

Chapter 8

A GARDEN IN A LAKE OF IM/POSSIBILITY

Photos by Sanna Irshad Mattoo

Text by Saiba Varma

In this visual ethnographic poem, we explore a centuries-old feminist and decolonial praxis of gardening on Dal Lake, one of Kashmir's most historically significant, but also most ecologically fragile tourist attractions, located in the heart of Srinagar city. Yet, rather than being a site of neglect, like other parts of Kashmir, the Dal is a victim of overinvestment (Varma 2020). The region's distended conflict has coincided with environmental concerns about protecting the lake, most notably the Dal Development Project, which created a foreshore road, promenades, and spaces for commercial and tourist activity (Bhan and Trisal 2017).

As the scale of the crisis became known, a number of civil society efforts to "save the Dal" mushroomed, although these often came at the expense of the concerns of lake dwellers themselves. While thousands of "boat people" continue to reside and make their living on the lake, their habitat and livelihoods are increasingly polluted, precarious and endangered.

Yet, on this dying lake, women lake dwellers maintain organic "floating" gardens, on which they grow a variety of seasonal vegetables. This visual ethnographic poem describes how this practice of gardening, of sustaining life in one of the world's most inhospitable places, constitutes a decolonial, feminist praxis of care. Through gardening, women exercise multiple forms of thought/attention/care (*khayal*): on themselves, their families, and the lake itself. This poem explores *khayal* and the interlocking scales that it brings into view as part of feminist and decolonial praxes in Kashmir.

***

The lake
     is choking.[1]

1. Starting in the 1970s and 1980s, many of the waterways that connected the Dal to other water bodies were blocked and concretized for road building due to ongoing urbanization.

No one can fight urbanization, land encroachment, pollution and
         a neverending conflict all at once.

Like transplants from another time and place,
         wooden boat-houses sit quietly in a row.

Some are worn,
         algae has nibbled their bottoms.

Others elegant,
         walnut carvings glossy in the sun.

The signs everywhere tell us to *Save Dal Lake. Please use a dustbin.*
         But no dustbin is big enough for millions of tonnes of raw sewage.[2]

It's not just the sewage. The lillies are choking the water too, says the boatman.
         Lillies are deceptively loving: heart-shaped, dew mounds, resting.

2. A 2016 study by researchers at Kashmir University found that only 20 percent of the
lake's water was clean, while 32 percent was severely degraded. At least fifteen large sewage
drains from the city empty into the 12 sq. km lake, releasing approximately 11 million
gallons of sewage and pollutants like phosphorus and nitrogen into the lake every day.

Weeds in disguise,
       stop oxygenation, fish flop belly up.

The boatman's oars help the lake breathe.
       Boat people are *the nutrient pumps in systems of circulation.*[3]

The lake is shrinking: thirty six percent in the last thirty seven years.
       At this rate, it'll be gone by 2086.

                     ***

It is not as if people have not tried
       to save the lake.

Maybe they tried too hard. In the 1970s and 1980s,
       more than 2600 lake dwellers were evicted.[4]

In 1997, a newly created government entity, the Lakes and Waterways
       Development Authority conserved by destroying.

3. Marya and Patel: 2021: 5.
4. Bhan and Trisal 2017.

They demolished the homes of lake dwellers and their cultivated gardens
    to reinvent Kashmir as an idyllic space of land and waterways.[5]

                                    ***

Rubia buries her face in her hands and giggles
        when we ask her about her garden on the water.

The garden pulls me away for an hour, or two, or four,
        she says, blushing, as if speaking of a lover.

She learned how to garden from her mother–and her mother's mother.
    I've been with the land since before I was born, she says.

I can spend all day in my garden
        if I get the chance.

She learned to cultivate vegetables on floating isthmuses of land,
        to nourish them with organic matter, thatched mats of mud and weeds.

5. Bhan and Trisal 2017.

This season, gourds, beans, cucumbers, tomatoes, collard greens, and spinach.
    In winter, she'll grow turnips, carrots, kohlrabi.

Rubia says the vegetables she grows on the water are pure.
    That's why we never get sick.

Rubia's son is educated, young, handsome. He wears John Lennon glasses.
    He shakes his head. He's a computer science major.

***

I wonder what allows Rubia's son to walk away
    while she remains drawn to the lake.

Subina, twenty, was also raised on the lake. She remembers a time
    when pashminas had their first wash in the waters of the Dal.

Though she still lives on the lake, now she *does not even put her hand in it,*
    she says. The lake has been dying her whole life.

She speaks of old wounds of racism, mud on her shoes,
    the scolding from her teachers, who knew she was a *boat person.*

***

Millions of dollars have been spent on saving Dal lake.
    Expensive dredging machines from Switzerland.

But the boat people say the machines
    don't pull weeds from the root. So they have only become stronger.

The boat people have their own techniques of dredging
    that are centuries-old.

In the resettlements, boat people
    were deemed the true pollutants.

The areas from where they have been evicted feel abandoned, desolate.
    The lake is dead.

The displacement of thousands for environmental protection.
  Blame those at the bottom of a social and caste hierarchy.

Meanwhile, *we are the children of Noah*, the boat people say.
  We are the gardeners of the lake.

Remove the gardeners
  and what happens to the garden?

***

Under the late morning sun,
  Rubia's garden is earthy and lush.

A peek of eggplant here,
  a heavily pregnant pumpkin there.

Blink–
  and you'll miss them.

For Rubia, gardening is not work, but *khayal*:
        a word that means to care and (at)tend, the embodied and sensory.

Khayal refers to the labor the garden requires,
        and what is needed to sustain her life, her family, and the lake itself.

Her garden is her love, and it gives in return
        a lifeworld, a way of life.

To care, in this way, is to decolonize:
        not to dismantle, but to create.

To keeping tending to
        a world falling to pieces.

To sprout new life,
        when everything around you is dying.

Bibliography

Bhan, Mona, and Nishita Trisal. "Fluid Landscapes, Sovereign Nature: Conservation and Counterinsurgency in Indian-Controlled Kashmir." *Critique of Anthropology* 37, no. 1 (2017): 67–92.

Marya, Rupa, and Raj Patel. *Inflamed: Deep Medicine and the Anatomy of Injustice*. New York: Farrar, Straus and Giroux, 2021.

Varma, Saiba. *The Occupied Clinic: Militarism and Care in Kashmir*. Durham and London: Duke University Press, 2020.

Chapter 9

QUYCA CHIAHAC CHIXISQUA (SOWING OURSELVES IN THE TERRITORY): EMBODIED EXPERIENCES OF INDIGENOUS URBAN GARDENS AND THE COLONIALITY OF NATURE

Andrea Sánchez-Castañeda, Erika Nivia, and Jorge Yopasá

Introduction

At the core of urban development, a foundational logic works to invisibilize Indigenous existence through the desecration of sacred and ancestral Indigenous places. Urbanization displaces, segregates, and assimilates Indigenous communities and erodes place-based epistemologies while subjecting urban Indigenous peoples to socioecological inequalities.[1] Although many urban Indigenous populations across the globe face similar circumstances, scholarship focused on the production of uneven urban environments has remained limited in the intersectional examinations on how ancestral Indigenous lands and urban Indigenous peoples factor into this equation.[2] Moreover, literature in the disciplines of anthropology and geography that focus on Indigenous issues has tended to focus either on rural Indigenous experiences of inequality[3] or Indigenous migration to major cities, with some noteworthy exceptions.[4]

These gaps in the literature on urban Indigenous issues are, to some extent, because most of the scholarship on urban indigeneity has been located in settler

---

1. Libby Porter, Julia Hurst, and Tina Grandinetti, 'The politics of greening unceded lands in the settler city', *Australian Geographer* 51, no. 2 (2020): 221–238.

2. Naama Blatman-Thomas, 'From transients to residents: urban Indigeneity in Israel and Australia', *Journal of Historical Geography* 58 (2017): 1–11; Julie Tomiak, 'Contesting the settler city: Indigenous self-determination, new urban reserves, and the neoliberalization of colonialism', *Antipode* 49, no. 4 (2017): 928-945; Michael Simpson and Jen Bagelman, 'Decolonizing urban political ecologies: The production of nature in settler colonial cities', *Annals of the American Association of Geographers* 108, no. 2 (2018): 558–568.

3. Sarah A Radcliffe, 'Gendered frontiers of land control: indigenous territory, women and contests over land in Ecuador', *Gender, Place & Culture* 21, no. 7 (2014): 854–871.

4. Philipp Horn, *Indigenous rights to the city: Ethnicity and urban planning in Bolivia and Ecuador*. (Routledge, 2019); Libby Porter and Oren Yiftachel, 'Urbanizing settler-colonial studies: Introduction to the special issue', *Settler Colonial Studies* 9, no. 2 (2019): 177–186.

colonial cities in the Global North, which display different realities to cities in the Global South,[5] where the legacy of colonialism remains present and is expressed through what has been coined the "coloniality of power."[6] The coloniality of power, or coloniality, refers to the logic and narratives that perpetuate and reproduce the supremacy of Eurocentric modern/colonial configurations and "all its dimensions: knowledge (epistemic), economic, political (military), aesthetic, ethical, subjective (race, sex), spiritual (religious)."[7] Similarly, literature in urban agriculture, either as a mechanism of neoliberal governance[8] or as a mechanism of resistance,[9] has focused on marginalized populations' experiences in the Global North—giving less attention to the racialized and gendered experiences in the Global South. For this reason, in this chapter, we aim to enrich this literature by presenting a case study of Indigenous urban gardens in Colombia's capital, Bogotá.

The adoption of the Political Constitution of 1991 marked a significant milestone as it acknowledged the cultural and political rights of Indigenous peoples by the Colombian state. Thereafter, the state recognized the Muysca people of Suba as the first urban Indigenous community and *cabildo*[10] in the nation. Although the Muysca reside in Suba, Bogotá, their status as urban Indigenous people does not stem from displacement from other regions of Colombia, as is the case with other ethnic communities. Instead, it corresponds to the fact that the capital city of Colombia was built around and engulfed their traditional town and sacred territory. The Muysca territory of Suba was primarily rural until the 1970s when it was quickly transformed by urbanization and incorporated into the capital city of Bogotá as a locality. In this regard, some authors have suggested that the harsh process of urbanization in Suba transformed the dynamic of the Muysca peoples and their territories:

5. Walter D. Mignolo and Catherine E. Walsh, '*On decoloniality: Concepts, analytics, praxis*'. Duke University Press, 2018.

6. Aníbal Quijano, 'Coloniality of power and Eurocentrism in Latin America', *International sociology* 15, no. 2 (2000): 215–232; Aníbal Quijano, 'Coloniality and modernity/rationality', Cultural studies 21, no. 2–3 (2007): 168–178; Aníbal Quijano. *Cuestiones y horizontes: de la dependencia histórico-estructural a la colonialidad/descolonialidad del poder*. CLACSO, 2020.

7. Mignolo and Walsh, On decoloniality, 141.

8. Rina Ghose and Margaret Pettygrove, 'Urban community gardens as spaces of citizenship', *Antipode* 46, no. 4 (2014): 1092–1112.

9. Mark Purcell and Shannon K. Tyman, 'Cultivating food as a right to the city" in *Urban gardening as politics*, ed. Chiara Tornaghi and Chiara Certomà (Routledge, 2018); Pierpaolo Mudu and Alessia Marini, 'Radical urban horticulture for food autonomy: Beyond the community gardens experience', *Antipode* 50, no. 2 (2018): 549–573.

10. An indigenous cabildo is "a special public entity, whose members are members of an indigenous community, elected and recognized by it, with a traditional socio-political organization, whose function is to legally represent the community, exercise authority and carry out the activities attributed by law, its uses, customs and the internal regulations of each community" (Ministerio del Interior 2013).

The houses in Suba used to have a plot in the middle where there used to be a crop or a garden; the average number of people living in a house was eight to ten. Nowadays, there are very few of these [type of] houses; Suba currently has more apartment buildings and gated communities. Some houses that began as a lot house had to reduce their space. However, some houses located in the center of [what used to be the town of] Suba still retain their original structure.[11]

Based on the Muysca's latest community census, 9,000 Muysca Indigenous peoples currently live in Suba; nevertheless, their traditional homes, which included spaces for cultivation, were gradually reduced to small home gardens or transformed into residential or commercial buildings. These changes in the landscape of Suba resonate with the words of the *mayoras* (Muysca women elders) Elizabeth "Chavelita" Sánchez-Caita and María Ozuna—during the series of interviews we conducted—who have kept a significant space inside their homes for growing food. These spaces, or *aulas vivas* [living classrooms] as many women have called them, because of their pedagogical function, have served as spaces for the revitalization of their language *Muysc cubun,* the revival of their traditional cultivations techniques and conservation of native plants, the preservation of their traditional healing practices, and the safeguarding of socioecological Indigenous systems in the city.

By drawing on decolonial theory and "epistemologies of the South" frameworks,[12] particularly the feminist notion of *Cuerpo-territorio* (body-territory), we examine how Muysca Indigenous women have challenged *the coloniality of nature,* or the exploitative logic materialized in socio-ecological inequalities, by cultivating and maintaining relationships with their land and their ancestors through the everyday practice of caring for their gardens in the city. In drawing on Native knowledge and experience, and collaborative ethnographic research framed within Participatory Action Research methodology with the Muysca Indigenous community of Suba in Bogotá, Colombia, we argue that in the Global South, Indigenous urban gardening is by nature an embodied, racialized, and gendered practice that helps create micro-geographies of resistance. In resonance with the visual ethnographic work presented by Saiba Varma and Sanna Irshad Mattoo, in this section of the book, our argument aims to shed light on the ongoing mechanisms through which gendered and racialized populations around the globe are practicing embodied-in-territory care, such as urban gardening, which challenges the forces of racial capitalism in urban environments.

As a collaborative piece, two people writing this paper are members of the Muysca Indigenous community of Suba: Erika Nivia is a graphic designer, and

11. Nicolas González Rojas, 'Poblando y Pensando Suba: Análisis de la influencia del proceso de urbanización de la localidad de Suba sobre las maneras de interactuar y la cotidianidad de sus primeros pobladores' (BA thesis., Facultad de Ciencias Sociales, Pontificia Universidad Javeriana, Bogotá, 2013).

12. Boaventura de Sousa Santos, *Epistemologies of the South: Justice against epistemicide* (Routledge, 2014).

Jorge Yopasá is a native anthropologist; both have worked from their disciplines and knowledges to strengthen the cultural process of the Muysca community through their research in their territory. Lastly, one of us, Andrea Sánchez-Castañeda, holds a PhD in anthropology and has worked with the Muysca of Suba since 2017, when she conducted fieldwork for her master's thesis. While Andrea is a nonindigenous Colombian citizen, she grew up in Suba and has focused her research on the process of resurgence and mechanisms of territorial appropriation of the Muysca people.

Cultivating Embodied Urban Natures

Urban gardens have been heralded for their emancipatory ability to create social capital and social networks around communal gardening,[13] providing green spaces in "highly uneven and deeply unjust urban landscapes,"[14] and re-envisioning noncapitalist relationships around the production of food.[15] Whereas some scholars in the Global South[16] have examined these spaces, the disciplines of anthropology and geography remain less engaged with the intersections in urban agriculture around the dimensions of race and gender. By the same token, while an urban political ecology approach has foregrounded experiences on the socioecological disparities in the production of urban landscapes, however, some scholars have identified the need to engage urban nature through the lenses of "antiracist, postcolonial and indigenous theory."[17] Recently, scholars have encountered this gap by contributing to, for instance, work on decolonizing practices in cities in the Global North.[18] This chapter aims to nourish a more

13. Jonathan Kingsley and Mardie Townsend, 'Dig in'to social capital: Community gardens as mechanisms for growing urban social connectedness', *Urban policy and research* 24, no. 4 (2006): 525–537; Catarina Passidomo, 'Community gardening and governance over urban nature in New Orleans's Lower Ninth Ward', *Urban Forestry & Urban Greening* 19 (2016): 271–277; Sara Shostak and Norris Guscott, '"Grounded in the Neighborhood, Grounded in Community": Social Capital and Health in Community Gardens', In *Food systems and health*, vol. 18, pp. 199–222. Emerald Publishing Limited, 2017; Søren Christensen, Pernille Malberg Dyg, and Kurt Allenberg, 'Urban community gardening, social capital, and" integration"–a mixed method exploration of urban" integration-gardening" in Copenhagen, Denmark', *Local Environment* 24, no. 3 (2019): 231–248.

14. Erik Swyngedouw and Nikolas C. Heynen. "Urban political ecology, justice and the politics of scale." *Antipode* 35, no. 5 (2003): 898–918.

15. Amanda DiVito Wilson, 'Beyond alternative: Exploring the potential for autonomous food spaces', *Antipode* 45, no. 3 (2013): 719–737.

16. Laura J. Shillington, 'Right to food, right to the city: Household urban agriculture, and socionatural metabolism in Managua, Nicaragua', *Geoforum* 44 (2013): 106.

17. Nik Heynen, 'Urban political ecology II: The abolitionist century', *Progress in Human Geography* 40, no. 6 (2016): 839.

18. Michael Simpson and Jen Bagelman, 'Decolonizing urban political ecologies, 2018.

"heterodox"[19] urban political ecology by foregrounding the racialized and gendered logic in the construction of the urban. Therefore, we want to expand the scope of urban agriculture and urban political ecology scholarship by using decolonial thinking from Latin America, particularly the Indigenous feminist notion of *Cuerpo-territorio* (body-territory).

The Maya-Xinka feminist scholar Lorena Cabnal affirms that defending the notion of *Cuerpo-territorio* (body-territory)[20] involves assuming the Indigenous human body as a historic territory in dispute with the colonial patriarchal power. According to Cabnal (2017), contesting, dignifying, and healing *Cuerpo-territorio* is an emancipatory political practice to defend Indigenous women and their territories. This reconceptualization of space as an extension of the body[21] acknowledges the relational nature of the relationship between Indigenous women and land as an ethical bond between "a group of humans, landscape and history."[22] Following the same train of thought, scholars have suggested that Indigenous peoples' bodies have been transgressed insofar as they are located and affected within racialized and colonized environments.[23]

In this chapter, we argue that the *urban coloniality of nature* is present in the discourses and practices of governance that degrade nature and prevent Indigenous peoples from living in more just environmental conditions, with access and rights not only to sacred natural sites but also to the everyday natural spaces where the community, in the process of revitalization of their identity, continues to re-create their cultural practices. The urban gardens are one of those everyday spaces where Indigenous peoples, in this case, Muysca Indigenous women, challenge the socioecological arrangements based on racialized urbanization processes. As an analytical tool, the notion of *Cuerpo-territorio* allows us to articulate a corporeal or embodied understanding of territory with the gendered and racialized practice of urban gardening cultivated by the Muysca women, as an everyday act of gender dynamics contestation, or what some scholars have called "tactics of de-subjectivation."[24]

19. Nik Heynen, 'Urban political ecology II: The abolitionist century', 842.

20. Lorena Cabnal, 'TZK'AT, Red de sanadoras ancestrales del feminismo comunitario desde Iximulew-Guatemala', *Ecología política* (2017): 98–102.

21. Elizabeth Sweet and Sara Ortiz Escalante, 'Engaging territorio cuerpo-tierra through body and community mapping: A methodology for making communities safer', *Gender, Place & Culture* 24, no. 4 (2017): 594–606

22. Juan A. Echeverri, 'Territory as body and territory as nature: Intercultural dialogue' in *The Land Within: Indigenous Territory and the Perception of Environment and the Perception of Environment*, ed. Alexandre Surrallés and Pedro Garcia Hierro (2005): 230–247.

23. Rob Nixon, *Slow Violence and the Environmetalism of the Poor* (Harvard University Press, 2011); Ann Laura Stoler, *Duress: Imperial durabilities in our times* (Duke University Press, 2016).

24. Escobar, *Territories of Difference*, Duke University Press, 2008.

The Production of Racialized Urban Environments

The territory is a vital element of the culture of Indigenous peoples, and its deterioration represents a threat to the survival of their ways of life and cultural heritage. In the case of the Muysca of Suba, the territorial arrangements and, later on, urban planning policies historically imposed in these lands have been the cause of the continuous degradation of the territory. Since the arrival of the colonial power of the Spanish Crown in the sixteenth century, the Indigenous territories were delimited, and the institution of the *resguardos* (colonial Indigenous reservations) was established, fragmenting the existing territorial relations between the native population and their traditional lands.

Land dispossession experienced by the Muysca people worsened in the nineteenth century with the independence and the establishment of the Republic of Colombia, which generated new territorial policies that dissolved the *resguardos* since the State saw collective Indigenous land property as a ballast for the "development" of the nation. From the nineteenth century until the latest decade of the twentieth century, many new nation-states promoted an Indigenous assimilation agenda called *mestizaje* throughout Latin America. Through this cultural homogenization project, the states advocated for eliminating ethnocultural differences under the ideology of economic progress. An example of this exclusionary ambition can be appreciated in one of the lectures given by former Colombian president Laureano Gómez:

> The other savage race, the indigenous from the American land, the second of the barbarous elements of our civilization, has transmitted to their descendants the fear of their defeat. In the rancour of defeat, [the race] seems to have taken refuge in taciturn dissimulation and insincere and malicious slyness. [The race] affects a complete indifference to the palpitations of national life, it seems resigned to misery and insignificance. [The race] is drugged by the sadness of the desert, intoxicated with the melancholy of its moorlands and its forests.[25]

In addition to this state-led assimilation program, in the 1950s, Suba, which used to be a small town—but an independent municipality—was incorporated as a locality in the capital city of Bogotá, which exacerbated the impacts on the territorial dynamics of the community. While the Muysca community was recognized as the first urban Indigenous community in Colombia—through the constitutional change in 1991—the state continues to fail the Muysca people in their right to obtain land rights.

In this context, the abrupt transformation from a rural to an urban landscape experienced by the community transformed the productive vocation of the land

---

25. Laureano Gómez, 'Los textos históricos: Interrogantes sobre el progreso de Colombia', *Boletín Cultural y Bibliográfico*, January 1981, 5–30.

Figure 17 *Tun Tâ*: Chavelita's garden is surrounded by urbanization. In the picture, Chavelita and Jorge Yopasá are working in the garden 2021. Photograph by Andrea Sánchez.

from its agricultural nature to developable land through political and spatial arrangements that rendered invisible the particularities of the territory and its original Muysca inhabitants. For example, throughout her lifetime, Chavelita, a woman who owns one of the urban gardens *Tun Tâ* (Figure 1), whom we interviewed, expressed her concern about the different threats to their land and their livelihood, attesting to how the land of Suba was repurposed from its agricultural nature to a highly urbanized and densely populated environment. During our conversation, Chavelita asserted:

> [The urbanisation] has affected us in various ways. The first way is through high taxes. Here, my territory is labelled as a *lote de engorde* (vacant lot) [...] Several of my relatives sold or parcelled their houses [...] *te quieren cobrar hasta la risa* [they (the authorities) want to charge you even for laughing]. Now it is all brick; there is no land to sow.[26]

Unexpectedly, as the Muysca women mentioned during our interview, one way the State continues to execute violent epistemic and spatial segregation of urban Indigenous communities, such as the Muysca de Suba community, is through

26. Interview with Elizabeth 'Chavelita' Sánchez Caita, October 22, 2022.

urban policies that prevent real estate speculation. The Department of Housing of the city of Bogotá imposes a high tax rate on undeveloped land as a strategy to discourage the accumulation and unproductive possession of the land by private owners. In this regard, land productivity is measured by its capacity to produce economic profit, mainly through the development of residential or commercial infrastructure, in contrast to its sacred and socio-ecological capacity experienced by the Muysca people.

Although these policies have been designed to prevent landowners and developers from playing with commercial values, they have negatively impacted the Indigenous Muyscas of Suba, who conserve space on their land to plant crops. In this sense, the Muyscas are treated in the same way as a construction company or a land speculator, which has caused high taxation, forcing the Indigenous people to destroy their orchards, sell their lots, go to other places in the city, or even to other parts of the country. Despite the urban planning policies imposed, many Muysca families have maintained their agricultural practices and way of life.

Muysca Tâ: *Muysca Gendered Urban Gardens and the Decoloniality of the Urban Space*

Urban gardens serve as vital agents in areas where socioeconomic inequalities are manifested in health disparities, where there is limited or no access to organic food, and lack of educational and green public spaces due to urbanization. Scholars[27] have suggested that Indigenous women play a crucial role in maintaining "food security, biodiversity conservation, and territorial appropriation."[28] In this sense, protecting urban gardens in the hands of the Muysca women is essential in these endeavors.

The Muisca gardens are one way Indigenous women contribute to urban agriculture. This experience can be explained due to historically women's central role of women in the care and cultivation of the Indigenous gardens of *pancoger* (Colombian term for subsistence agriculture), which in the native Muysca language is called *tâ*. Although the traditional extensive agriculture systems, such as the cultivation ridges and the terraces called *Sunas* and *Sincas* have been replaced by modern practices and technologies, the gardens cared for by women and located inside the lots of the houses have been maintained, demonstrating the vital role of the Muysca woman in the production of food for the family.

Despite the difficulties and adversities the Muysca gardens led by women have faced, these spaces have survived as a relic of traditional knowledge and practices. The women who lead these gardens have reproduced seeds for generations, making them *sabedoras* (connoisseurs) and guardians of a living seed bank. These seeds can be considered a metaphor for the Muysca culture, which continues to grow in

---

27. Arturo, Escobar, *Territories of Difference*.
28. Ibid., 236.

a city full of cement. In the context of increasing urbanization and environmental degradation, Indigenous gardens signify the importance of maintaining and strengthening traditional cultural and agricultural practices.

Based on our conversation with Indigenous women, losing these spaces makes territorial defense and knowledge sharing difficult. It also breaks with deep learning processes that favored collective work. For instance, Muyscas Rodolfo and Ligia Nivia, siblings who have directly witnessed the territorial transformations due to the urbanization of Suba, remarked that: "the youth nowadays don't even know what a mint is, what stems are, they don't know what a cilantro is. Nothing, because right now there is nowhere to teach them."[29] In like manner, María Angélica Cabiativa, a young woman who maintains a vegetable garden with her family, stated the following:

[the urbanisation] makes the revitalisation process somewhat difficult. Our culture is the community, and since we are not so [physically] close anymore and do not have our own communal spaces, such as the *aulas vivas* (living classrooms) in these gardens, [there are] no places to carry out these traditional activities and to which we should revitalise. Furthermore, if we want to reinvigorate our culture, [this, the lack of communal places] makes that even more difficult.[30]

The communal gardens have been meeting and learning places where knowledge is transmitted and practices for sustainability are developed. In our conversations, Maria showed concern about the relationship between the loss of these spaces and the loss of traditional knowledge that had weakened the community's cultural identity. Nevertheless, despite the inevitable threats that have emerged with urbanization, women have maintained thriving urban garden spaces that resist and function as what the community has referred to as *aulas vivas* (living classrooms). As Angela Niviayo from the *Niviayo Tâ* garden (Figure 2) states: "The Muysca gardens in Suba are rural laboratories of resistance within the city."[31] These spaces generate pedagogies that strengthen territorial ties and promote the recovery of ancestral knowledge. For instance, in the path toward the revitalization of sacred practices, both the women in charge of the gardens, as other elders and traditional healers, have engaged with the cultivation, harvest, and consumption of sacred plant medicines that once were forbidden and demonized since colonization. In this regard, entheogens or sacred plant medicines such as tobacco, cannabis, *borrachero* (*Brugmansia* tree), coca, and their derivatives, have come to play a central role in the Muisca process of Indigenous revitalization. Entheogens play a key role in ritual gatherings where the Muisca discuss efforts to reappropriate

29. Interview with Rodolfo and Ligia Nivia, February 16, 2022.

30. Interview with Maria Angelica Cabiativa January 29, 2022.

31. Interview with Angela Niviayo, February 16, 2022.

their traditional lands. They are also used as forms of ideological resistance and memory revitalization as they serve as catalysts for creating new meanings of their collective identity and relationship to the land.

These educational processes of cultural revitalization can be understood within the framework of the *Pedagogía de la Madre Tierra*[32] (Pedagogy of the Mother Earth), an Indigenous episteme that recognizes the importance of the territory as a living and sacred being. For instance, during the March equinox that marks the beginning of the Muysca year, the community carries out a ritual called the "seed blessing," in which women, elders, and healers thank, prepare, and bestow the land in the garden to sow what is going to be harvested during the next equinox celebration. In September, the equinox of harvest or what the Muysca refer to as the Flower celebration or the *Huitaca* girl celebration—honoring the Muysca goddess—the community celebrates the harvest of the year and the women's transition from childhood to womanhood. Both of these rituals are an embodied testimony of the connection that the Muysca have with their territory and their sacred and traditional practices. These gardens are spaces where food is grown sustainably, knowledge is shared, and collective work is promoted; they are also a sample of the resistance of the communities against the processes of dispossession and loss of cultural identity.

Figure 18 *Niviayo Tâ*: Angela's garden 2021. Photograph by Erika Nivia.

32. Abadio Green Stócel, 'Significados de Vida: Espejo De Nuestra Memoria En Defensa De La Madre Tierra' (Doctoral Diss., Universidad de Antioquia, Medellín, 2011).

Muysca Gardens as aulas vivas *for Language Revival*

Conserving the Muysca urban gardens also contributes to the process of linguistic revitalization, a cornerstone of efforts to preserve the Muysca culture and its legacy. This linguistic revitalization process represents an inspiring example of how communities can claim their roots and cultural identity in the face of the globalizing homogenization that characterizes our era. As *aulas vivas*, these gardens have served as places of cultural resurgence for the Muysca people. As an everyday in-place act of resurgence among the Muyscas, revitalizing their language is considered a radical historical act in a context in which their language, *Muysc cubun*, has been labeled as extinct. The revitalization of ancestral languages is part of the guarantee of defense of the cultural rights of Indigenous peoples in Colombia, recognized in Law 1381 of 2010. The existence of colonial manuscripts with unique vocabularies, such as *Manuscript 2922* at the Royal Library of Madrid or the anonymous *Manuscript 158* at the National Library of Colombia, have been crucial in the process of language revitalization.

In these gardens, women have kept alive many words of Muysca origin, making these spaces of great cultural importance. In this regard, one of the most noteworthy linguists in the Muysca language, the Colombian scholar Diana Andrea Giraldo Gallego, argues that "the semantic fields for *field*, *crop*, and *animals*[33] represent a little more than three quarters (77 percent) of the total lexemes [smallest unit of meaning in a word] of Muysca origin or of possible Muysca origin registered."[34] In addition, Muysca women continue to recognize food plants in these gardens by their Muysca names, for instance, *cubio* (*Tropaeolum tuberosum*), *guasca* (*Galinsoga parviflora* or potato weed), and *uchuva* (*Physalis peruviana* or golden berry), among others.

A remarkable example of this process of language recovery in-place is the *Muysca* term for garden, which in the ancestral language, the *Muysc cubun,* is known as "tâ." The word *tâ* has several meanings, including "where food supplies are grown" and "gardens of subsistence farming"; even the etymology of the word Bogotá—the name of the capital city—translates as "a field of gardens." This word has gained relevance in the daily life of the Muyscas of Suba, who have found in this word a connection with their territory and with their cultural practices. Therefore, revitalizing the Muysca language not only implies a recovery of terms but also becomes an exercise of resistance and cultural affirmation in the urban context where multiple social and political tensions occur.

Another crucial aspect of the linguistic revitalization undertaken by the Muyscas of Suba is the recovery of their cultural concepts that allow them to reflect on their world experience. For instance, two concepts of importance for this work have been recovered: *muysca* and *muysquyn*, which translate as "human" and "nature," respectively. The linguistic closeness of these words reveals a Muysca

33. The words 'fields, crop, and animals' have been italicized by the authors.

34. Diana Andrea Giraldo Gallego, 'Préstamos de origen Muisca en Cundinamarca y Boyacá', 131.

ontology in which the human being is intrinsically related to nature since the human is part of it. This approach of interdependence and harmony between human beings and nature can contrast with the conception of urban policies that are built solely through the human experience, leaving aside other forms of life. *Muysquyn* refers to "what grows, develops, and it is transformed," and so, in the gardens, the bodies are an extension of the territory. As a "decolonized embodied ontology,"[35] using *cuerpo-territorio* [body-territory] has allowed us to understand how the Muysca community and Suba, as their territory, are a single subject that contests hegemonic epistemologies that aim to obliterate Indigenous alternative corporeal and ethical dispositions.

The Muysca gardens contribute to the growth and reproduction of the natural world, and their crops favor the sustenance of the human being, maintaining a reciprocal relationship where all beings are permanently feeling, growing, transforming, developing, and interacting. Hence, the revitalization of these Muysca concepts has allowed the community to rebuild their cultural identity and strengthen their relationship with its natural environment, which in turn has generated a deep awareness of what gardens mean as spaces of reproduction of what grows, including for human beings, the Muysca, who grow the same as their gardens.

Conclusion

As a result of the reproduction of racial imaginaries that situate Indigenous bodies in particular landscapes such as rural environments, native peoples such as the Muysca of Suba continue to be culturally obliterated, segregated, and displaced from their ancestral lands. As we have shown through the case of the Muysca, the Colombian state used assimilation techniques to render Indigenous people invisible in cities, facilitating urban development on sacred and traditional territories. In this sense, we have argued that colonial violence is exerted by urban planning policies that are materialized in the implementation of socioecological arrangements that restrict and prevent Indigenous communities' access to their natural sacred sites.

The Muysca gardens cared for by women are a sample of the importance of traditional agriculture and the crucial role women have historically played in food production, seed conservation, and the preservation of important ecological spaces in the city. The abolitionist and decolonial future we present in this chapter is not only a creation for the future but is a practice of decolonization currently taking place in a city in the Global South. These urban gardens are not only crucial for the food security of the communities but are also a form of cultural resistance

---

35. Lindsay Naylor, Michelle Daigle, Sofia Zaragocin, Margaret Marietta Ramirez, and Mary Gilmartin, 'Interventions: Bringing the decolonial to *political geography*', Political Geography, 66 (2018): 199–209.

in an increasingly homogeneous world. Therefore, we argue that it is essential to recognize and value the knowledge and experience of the women who lead these gardens and promote their participation in decision-making spaces and the management of urban public policies, consider Indigenous place-based ontologies, and the territory's particularities, in order to guarantee the right to a dignified and sustainable life for these communities.

Bibliography

Blatman-Thomas, Naama. "From Transients to Residents: Urban Indigeneity in Israel and Australia." *Journal of Historical Geography* 58 (2017): 1–11.

Cabnal, Lorena. "TZK'AT, Red de sanadoras ancestrales del feminismo comunitario desde Iximulew-Guatemala." *Ecología política* 54 (2017): 98–102.

Christensen, Søren, Pernille Malberg Dyg, and Kurt Allenberg. "Urban Community Gardening, Social Capital, and 'Integration'—A Mixed Method Exploration of Urban 'Integration-Gardening' in Copenhagen, Denmark." *Local Environment* 24, no. 3 (2019): 231–48.

Dorries, Heather, David Hugill, and Julie Tomiak. "Racial Capitalism and the Production of Settler Colonial Cities." *Geoforum*, 2019.

Echeverri, Juan A. "Territory as Body and Territory as Nature: Intercultural Dialogue." In *The Land within: Indigenous Territory and the Perception of Environment and the Perception of Environment*, edited by Alexandre Surrallés and Pedro Garcia Hierro, 230–47. Copenhagen: IWGIA, 2005.

Escobar, Arturo. *Territories of Difference*. Durham, NC: Duke University Press, 2008.

Ghose, Rina, and Margaret Pettygrove. "Urban Community Gardens as Spaces of Citizenship." *Antipode* 46, no. 4 (2014): 1092–112.

Giraldo Gallego, and Diana Andrea. "Prestamos de origen muisca en Cundinamarca y Boyaca." *Estudios de Lingüística Chibcha* 31 (2012): 93–148.

Gómez, Laureano. "Los textos históricos: Interrogantes sobre el progreso de Colombia." *Boletín Cultural y Bibliográfico* 18, no. 1 (1981): 5–30.

Gonzales Rojas, Nicolas. "Poblando y Pensando Suba: Análisis de la influencia del proceso deurbanización de la localidad de Suba sobre las maneras de interactuar y la cotidianidad de sus primeros pobladores." BA thesis., Facultad de Ciencias Sociales, Pontificia Universidad Javeriana, Bogotá, 2013.

Green Stócel, Abadio. "Significados de Vida: Espejo De Nuestra Memoria En Defensa De La Madre Tierra." Doctoral Diss., Universidad de Antioquia, Medellín, 2011.

Heynen, Nik. "Urban Political Ecology II: The Abolitionist Century." *Progress in Human Geography* 40, no. 6 (2016): 839–45.

Horn, Philipp. *Indigenous Rights to the City: Ethnicity and Urban Planning in Bolivia and Ecuador*. Abingdon: Routledge, 2019.

Kingsley, Jonathan, and Mardie Townsend. "'Dig in' to Social Capital: Community Gardens as Mechanisms for Growing Urban Social Connectedness." *Urban Pol. Res* 24, (2006): 525–37.

Mignolo, Walter D., and Catherine E. Walsh. *On Decoloniality: Concepts, Analytics, Praxis*. Durham, NC: Duke University Press, 2018.

Mudu, Pierpaolo, and Alessia Marini. "Radical Urban Horticulture for Food Autonomy: Beyond the Community Gardens Experience." *Antipode* 50, no. 2 (2018): 549–73.

Naylor, Lindsay, Michelle Daigle, Sofia Zaragocin, Margaret Marietta Ramírez, and Mary Gilmartin. "Interventions: Bringing the Decolonial to Political Geography." *Political Geography* 66 (2018): 199–209.

Oslender, Ulrich. "Geographies of the Pluriverse: Decolonial Thinking and Ontological Conflict on Colombia's Pacific Coast." *Annals of the American Association of Geographers* 109, no. 6 (2019): 1691–705.

Passidomo, Catarina. "Community Gardening and Governance over Urban Nature in New Orleans's Lower Ninth Ward." *Urban Forestry & Urban Greening* 19 (2016): 271–7.

Porter, Libby, and Oren Yiftachel. "Urbanizing Settler-Colonial Studies: Introduction to the Special Issue." *Settler Colonial Studies* 9, no. 2 (2019): 177–86.

Porter, Libby, Julia Hurst, and Tina Grandinetti. "The Politics of Greening Unceded Lands in the Settler City." *Australian Geographer* 51, no. 2 (2020): 221–38.

Purcell, Mark, and Shannon K. Tyman. "Cultivating Food as a Right to the City." In *Urban Gardening as Politics*, edited by Chiara Tornaghi and Chiara Certomà, 62–81. New York: Routledge, 2018.

Quijano, Anibal. "Coloniality of Power and Eurocentrism in Latin America." *International Sociology* 15, no. 2 (2000): 215–32.

Quijano, Aníbal. "Coloniality and Modernity/Rationality." *Cultural Studies* 21, no. 2–3 (2007): 168–78.

Quijano, Aníbal. *Cuestiones y horizontes: de la dependencia histórico-estructural a la colonialidad/descolonialidad del poder*. CLACSO, 2020.

Radcliffe, Sarah A. "Gendered Frontiers of Land Control: Indigenous Territory, Women and Contests over Land in Ecuador." *Gender, Place & Culture* 21, no. 7 (2014): 854–71.

Santos, Boaventura de Sousa. *Epistemologies of the South: Justice against Epistemicide*. Boulder: Paradigm, 2014.

Shillington, Laura J. "Right to Food, Right to the City: Household Urban Agriculture, and Socionatural Metabolism in Managua, Nicaragua." *Geoforum* 44 (2013): 103–11.

Shostak, Sara, and Norris Guscott. "'Grounded in the Neighborhood, Grounded in Community': Social Capital and Health in Community Gardens." In *Food Systems and Health*, edited by Sara Shostak, vol. 18, 199–222. Bingley: Emerald Publishing Limited, 2017.

Simpson, Michael, and Jen Bagelman. "Decolonizing Urban Political Ecologies: The Production of Nature in Settler Colonial Cities." *Annals of the American Association of Geographers* 108, no. 2 (2018): 558–68.

Sweet, Elizabeth, and Sara Ortiz Escalante. "Engaging Territorio Cuerpo-Tierra through Body and Community Mapping: A Methodology for Making Communities Safer." *Gender, Place & Culture* 24, no. 4 (2017): 594–606.

Swyngedouw, Erik, and Nikolas C. Heynen. "Urban Political Ecology, Justice and the Politics of Scale." *Antipode* 35, no. 5 (2003): 898–918.

Tomiak, Julie. "Contesting the Settler City: Indigenous Self-Determination, New Urban Reserves, and the Neoliberalization of Colonialism." *Antipode* 49, no. 4 (2017): 928–45.

Wilson, Amanda DiVito. "Beyond Alternative: Exploring the Potential for Autonomous Food Spaces." *Antipode* 45, no. 3 (2013): 719–37.

CONTRIBUTORS

Alexia Arani (she/they) is an Assistant Professor of Women's, Gender and Queer Studies at California Polytechnic State University, San Luis Obispo. Her teaching and research interests in queer/trans of color critique, prison abolition, and disability justice are informed by her work as a mutual aid organizer, political educator, and scholar-activist.

Andrea Sánchez-Castañeda is a lecturer of anthropology at Florida International University. She incorporates Participatory Action Research and decolonial feminist methodologies into her research in the fields of urban indigeneity and urban political ecology.

Bhasha Chakrabarti is a multi-genre artist whose work explores global conversations of face, gender and power, including between feminine forms of labor from the global South and resistance movements of marginalized communities in the global North. She graduated with an MFA in Painting and Printmaking from the Yale School of Art in 2022.

Isabelle Higgins is a PhD candidate in the Department of Sociology, University of Cambridge. Her research focuses on exploring how racial, reproductive, and digital injustices are reproduced through everyday online practices.

Kristine Amanda Koyama is a PhD candidate in English at the University of Wisconsin-Milwaukee, where they also teach composition, research, and literature courses. They research nineteenth-century literature and social justice movements, particularly through texts that rely on depictions of children and animals to catalyze civic engagement and social movements.

Poh Lin Lee is a narrative therapy practitioner, social worker, co-researcher of trauma/displacement, writer, teacher, film protagonist, and film/creative consultant. She is a member of the teaching faculty of Dulwich Centre Australia, Re-authoring Teaching USA and an honorary clinical fellow of the School of Social Work, University of Melbourne. She is dedicated to crafting gatherings and questions that offer anti-oppressive pathways, movements, and possibilities in projects and practices across diverse fields.

Mika Lillit Lior is an interdisciplinary dance artist-scholar and a postdoctoral fellow at York University in Toronto. Foregrounding oral history-making practices and local constructions of gender and sexuality, Lior's research addresses ritual choreographies and their political valences in Bahia, Brazil. She holds a PhD in Culture and Performance from the University of California, Los Angeles.

Inshah Malik is an Associate Professor of Politics at the School of Politics and Diplomacy, New Vision University. She is a political theorist and an ethnographer by training. Her book *Muslim Women, Agency and Resistance Politics: The Case of Kashmir* was published in 2019 by Palgrave Macmillan. She is also a former Fox International Fellow at Yale University.

Sanna Irshad Mattoo is a photojournalist and documentary photographer based in Indian-administered Kashmir. Sanna is the winner of the 2022 Pulitzer Prize in feature photography. She has been a Magnum Foundation grantee (2022) for their counter-histories initiative and a Photography and Social Justice Fellow 2021. She contributes to Reuters as a multimedia journalist.

Erika Nivia is a native woman from Suba (Bogotá, Colombia) belonging to the Muysca Indigenous community of Suba, and she is a graphic designer from the National University of Colombia. Her interest in the use of design for identity strengthening has led her to work for the National Indigenous Organization of Colombia (ONIC) in the communications area of nongovernmental organizations that promote the autonomy of ethnic communities.

Carolyn Ureña is the Director of Academic Advising in the College of Arts and Sciences at the University of Pennsylvania. Her research has focused on the clinical, philosophical, and political writings of the revolutionary Black psychiatrist Frantz Fanon. A multilingual comparatist by training, her writing has appeared in *Bandung: Journal of the Global South*, *Disability and the Global South*, *Hypatia: A Journal of Feminist Philosophy*, *Revista de Estudios Hispánicos*, and *History of Photography*.

Saiba Varma is an Associate Professor of Anthropology at the University of California, San Diego. Trained as a medical and psychological anthropologist, she is the author of *The Occupied Clinic: Militarism in Care in Kashmir* (Duke University Press, 2020), which won the Edie Turner Prize for Ethnographic Writing from the American Anthropological Association.

Xiaolu Wang documents, curates, translates, maps interiority, mixes video, poetry, memory, translations, and a decolonial lens. They seek, are, host, read, and fly kites. Suspended between places and metaphorical landscapes, they listen for cat purrs and warm spells.

Mardiya Siba Yahaya is a community manager at Team Community, a project of Article 19. She is a feminist digital sociologist whose work wrangles between political and community violence and shifting power dynamics in techno-societies. She experiments with digital justice approaches toward building public interest technologies with local communities.

Jorge Yopasá is a weaver and native anthropologist of the Muysca people from Suba in Bogotá, Colombia. His research interest has led him to participate in the research group of the Muysca language (Muysccubun), where he has been involved in the process of linguistic revitalization using textile art as a language. His work has been presented at international conferences such as the Second International Crafts Congress in Mexico.

INDEX